Meredith Levy   Noel Goodey   Diana Goodey

Messages

Workbook

4

T0349688

My name is ....

I am in Class ....

The name of my school is ....

My English teacher is ....

My address is ....

....

....

Date ....

CAMBRIDGE
UNIVERSITY PRESS

1 Getting together

1 The present and the past G→ 1, 2, 8a

Underline the verbs in the text and then write them in the correct list: Present or Past.

Martin <u>loves</u> old films. He watches them on DVD. Yesterday he bought *The Third Man,* and he's watching it at the moment. The British film director Carol Reed made the film in 1949. The English writer Graham Greene wrote the story and Orson Welles, the great American actor, played the main role. A lot of people think it was the best British film of the 20th century. The action takes place in the Austrian capital, Vienna, in the 1940s. *The Third Man* is very exciting, full of mystery and surprise. Martin is really enjoying it.

Alexander Korda & David O. Selznick present
A London Film Production
JOSEPH
COTTEN
VALLI
ORSON
WELLES
TREVOR
HOWARD
in
CAROL REED'S
production
THE *THIRD* MAN
by Graham Greene
Distributed by British Lion Film Corpn. Ltd.

Present

...........loves...........   ....

....

....

....

Past

....

....

....

2 What's happening? G→ 2

This picture is called *Welcome!* It shows a scene in a London café in the 1960s.
Complete the description of the picture. Use the verbs in the box in the present continuous.

wear	sit (x 2)	eat	laugh	drink
~~come~~	wash	look at	carry	play

A woman ¹ __is coming__ into the café. She
² .... a dark suit and a big
hat. She ³.............................. a dog under her
arm. Two men ⁴.............................. at a table
near the window. They ⁵..............................
cards. Two teenage girls ⁶..............................
ice cream. They ⁷.............................. . A man
⁸ .... at a table near the
counter. He ⁹.............................. coffee. The
café owner ¹⁰.............................. cups and
plates behind the counter. They ¹¹..............................
all .... the woman with the dog.

3 Reading *The fans are still crying*

Read the text about Elvis Presley. Then read the sentences and write *T* (true) or *F* (false) or *?* (the answer isn't in the text).

There's a long queue of people outside Graceland, a large house in Memphis, Tennessee.

This was the home of Elvis Presley, a man who, in the 1950s, changed popular music for ever. In 1956 he recorded a song called *Heartbreak Hotel*, and when young people heard it they were amazed.

His style of music was new and exciting. Suddenly, everyone wanted to listen to rock and roll and, thanks to Elvis Presley, it spread all over the world.

Hundreds of fans are here this morning. Some of them are carrying photos of Elvis; some of them are listening to his music on their headphones; some of them are crying. Every year thousands of people visit Graceland to say their personal goodbye to the man they call 'the King'.

When he left school, Elvis became a truck driver. Then in 1954 he started to make records. He was tall, dark and good-looking. Girls fell in love with him. Boys wanted to look like him – they copied his hairstyle and the way he moved.

During the last years of his life Elvis's health wasn't good. He died of a heart attack in 1977 when he was only 42. But for many people he's still 'the King', and the fans are still crying.

1 Elvis lived at Graceland in Memphis. ....

2 Elvis created a different style of popular music. ....

3 There aren't many people in the queue. ....

4 All the fans are carrying photos of Elvis. ....

5 Elvis's first job wasn't as a singer. ....

6 He made hundreds of records. ....

7 He ate very unhealthy food. ....

8 He wasn't very old when he died. ....

4 A biography

Imagine you're Gemma Finch. Write sentences, using your fact file.

FACT FILE

NAME: Gemma Finch
DATE OF BIRTH: 1976   PLACE OF BIRTH: London
PROFESSION: Writer

- Worked for BBC Television (1998 – 2001)
- Most famous book: *Alone in the City* (2005)
- Present project: a book about children in China

My name's ¹.................. . I'm a ².................. .

I'm ³.................. years old. I ⁴.................. in London.

I ⁵.................. BBC Television for ⁶.................. years.

I ⁷.................. my most famous book, *Alone in the City,* ⁸.................. 2005.

At the moment I ⁹.................. a book about children in China.

5 Extension

Word game

Add the first and the last letter to make complete nouns.

1 UITA   *GUITAR*

2 OSTCAR ....

3 ICKE ....

4 RIEN ....

5 CTO ....

6 INGE ....

7 AITE ....

8 OUNTE ....

1 Key vocabulary *Verbs + prepositions*   26

Write the sentences in a different way. Use the verbs in brackets + the correct preposition
(*about, at, for, from* or *to*).

1 She often has a conversation with her neighbour.   (*talk*) She often *talks to her neighbour* .

2 When they talk about pop music, they never agree.   (*argue*) They always _____ .

3 I'm trying to find my bag.   (*look*) I'm _____ .

4 Shall I show you my holiday photos?   (*look*) Do you want to _____ ?

5 Yasuko is from Japan.   (*come*) Yasuko _____ .

6 Tom always turns on the radio at 7 o'clock.   (*listen*) Tom always _____ .

7 I want an answer and I'm waiting.   (*wait*) I'm _____ .

8 I can't forget you!   (*think*) I _____ every day.

2 Present continuous: affirmative and negative   2

Complete the sentences. Use the affirmative or the negative form of the present continuous.

1 Jack isn't listening to the teacher because he *'s thinking* (*think*) about his new computer game.

2 I _____ (*enjoy*) this party very much. Shall we go home?

3 Kate's friends _____ (*wait*) for her because she isn't ready.

4 I'm looking for my mobile, but you _____ (*help*) me!

5 Harry's mum is trying to choose a jacket for him, but he _____ (*look*) at the jackets.

He _____ (*look*) at the DVDs.

3 Present continuous: questions and short answers   2

Make questions in the present continuous and complete the short answers.

① A: I/hurt/you?

Am I hurting you?

B: Yes, *you are.*

② A: you/make/a cake?

_____

B: Yes, _____ .

③ A: we/move?

_____

B: No, _____ .

④ A: the rain/come in?

_____

B: Yes, _____ .

⑤ A: your brother/win?

_____

B: No, _____ .

⑥ A: they/play well?

_____

B: No, _____ .

4 Verbs + prepositions: questions with *What* and *Who* Ⓖ➔ 26

Ask these people questions. Use *What* or *Who* + verb + preposition. Use verbs from Exercise 1.

What are you listening to?

5 Key expressions *Contradictions* Ⓖ➔ 29

Complete the conversations. A contradicts B each time.

1 A: Ugh! This pizza's terrible.
   B: No, it isn't!

   A: *Yes, it is!* It's awful.

2 A: I'm 17.
   B: No, you aren't!

   A: .... ! It was my birthday yesterday.

3 A: You've got my sunglasses.
   B: No, I haven't!

   A: .... ! They're mine.

4 A: Sarah doesn't play volleyball.
   B: Yes, she does!

   A: .... ! She plays hockey.

6 Listening *What are they talking about?*

🔊 Listen to the three conversations. Then answer these questions.

Conversation 1

1 What are they waiting for?

   ....

2 What time is it now?

   ....

Conversation 2

1 What are they looking at?

   ....

2 Is the girl in Paris now?

   ....

Conversation 3

1 Where are they?

   ....

2 What are they looking for?

   ....

7 Extension *A puzzle*

Look at the picture and read the sentences. Can you find the boys' names?

Leo's wearing glasses. Rob isn't eating.
Max and Rob aren't wearing baseball
caps. Charlie isn't talking on his
mobile. Leo and Dave aren't reading.

A = ...

B = ...

C = ...

D = ...

E = ...

'Postcards': Vocabulary check

1 Look at the words in the box. Can you find four nouns?

full moon	halfway	headphones	low
it sounds	nice and warm	right now
sunset	I wonder	tour

....

....

2 Complete the sentences. Use the words in the box in Exercise 1.

1 New York was wonderful. We got a bus and did a

.... of Manhattan.

2 It's a beautiful night. There's a ....

3 Dave has had an accident. I don't know what happened

but .... serious.

4 I can't talk to you .... I'm very busy.

5 Paul's on holiday. .... what he's

doing at the moment.

6 The lights in the club were .... and I

couldn't see very well.

7 There was a fabulous .... this

evening. The sky was red and gold.

8 A: That's a good coat for the winter.

B: Yes, it's ....

9 The stereo's too loud. Why don't you listen to your music

on your .... ?

10 The boat was in the middle of the Atlantic,

.... between England and America.

3 Translate these sentences into your language.

1 A: What are you looking for?

B: My keys. I think I left them on the counter at the sports shop.

....

....

....

....

2 A: The tickets are on the table.

B: No, they aren't. Where are they?

....

....

....

3 A: Sorry I'm late.

B: Hurry up! We're meeting Lisa outside the café at half past six.

....

....

....

....

4 Martin's living somewhere in Japan at the moment.

....

....

5 A: Look at Nick! He's wearing a suit and a tie.

B: You're joking! I wonder where he's going.

....

....

....

....

6 You aren't listening to me. You're thinking about something. What are you thinking about?

....

....

Unit 1 Learning diary

Date _____

Now I know how to:

	Easy	Not bad	Difficult

- use the present continuous to describe a picture. ☐ ☐ ☐

  The picture shows a scene in a café. A man and a woman _____ sitting at a table, but they _____ talking to each other. A waiter _____ working behind the counter.

- give a short biography of a famous person in the past. ☐ ☐ ☐

  James Dean was an American actor. He _____ born in 1931. He _____ three films. He _____ only 24 when he _____ in 1955.

- make questions with verbs + prepositions. ☐ ☐ ☐

  I'm waiting for someone.   Who are you waiting _____ ?

  I talked to some interesting people.   Who did you talk _____ ?

- contradict someone. ☐ ☐ ☐

  You never listen to me.   Yes, I do!

  You're scared.   No, _____ !

  You haven't got my address.   Yes, _____ !

- write a postcard. ☐ ☐ ☐

KEY WORDS

Verbs + prepositions

look at something	= _____ *(in my language)*
look for something	= _____
talk about something	= _____
think about something	= _____
wait for something	= _____
argue about something	= _____
come from (place of birth)	= _____

WORD WORK

some ..., every ...

some *one* _____

some _____

some _____

every _____

every _____

every *where* _____

1 Key vocabulary *Flats and houses*

Complete the text with words describing flats and houses.

I live with my family in a ¹b............................ of flats in London. We're lucky because our flat's on the ²g............................ floor, so we've got a little ³g............................ at the back. My dad grows vegetables there. We keep our car in a ⁴g............................ next to the flats. My friend Emma lives on the third ⁵f............................ . Her flat is really nice. It's got a ⁶b............................ , so in summer the family can sit outside in the sun. When I go to Emma's, I don't often use the ⁷l............................ because it's very slow. I usually go up the ⁸s............................ .

2 Present simple: questions and answers G→1

Look at the pictures and complete the questions and answers. Use the present simple.

1

Mill Street

2

3

4

5

6

1 (*Where/Kerry/live*)

   Where does Kerry live?

   She .... in .... Street.

2 (*she/live*)

   .... in a block of flats?

   .... , she ....

3 (*How/Kerry and her friends/get to school*)

   .... ?

   They ....

4 (*they/have lunch in the canteen*)

   ....

   .... ?

   .... , they ....

5 (*Where/Kerry/do her homework*)

   .... ?

   She .... it in her ....

6 (*Kerry/know her neighbours*)

   .... ?

   .... , she ....

3 Present simple or present continuous? G→ 1, 2

Peter's at home on Sunday morning. Underline the correct verb form.

1 It's Sunday morning, so I (*'m reading* / *read*) my music magazine in bed.
2 I (*don't get up* / *'m not getting up*) early at weekends.
3 I (*'m knowing* / *know*) everyone in our block of flats.
4 Our neighbours are Bosnian. They (*'re coming* / *come*) from Mostar.
5 It's sunny today and they (*have* / *'re having*) breakfast on their balcony.
6 My brother (*isn't owning* / *doesn't own*) a car. He's got a motorbike.
7 He (*cleans* / *'s cleaning*) his motorbike now.
8 He (*'s doing* / *does*) the same thing every Sunday morning.

4 Relative clauses with *who, that, which* G→ 30

Put the words in the right order and make sentences.

1 a / got / I'd / a / that's / house / garden / like / big

   I'd like a house that's got a big garden.

2 plays / he / the / that / the / is / trumpet / man ?

   _____

   _____

3 old / live / a / house / is / which / 300 years / we / in

   _____

   _____

4 shop / that / postcards / there / is / a / sells ?

   _____

   _____

5 overlooks / got / flat / that / the / she's / river / a

   _____

   _____

6 people / on / they / live / floor / are / the / ground / who / the ?

   _____

   _____

5 Listening *Definitions*

🔊 Listen to the four conversations. Tick (✓) the right picture: A, B or C.

1   A ☐   B ☐   C ☐

2   A ☐   B ☐   C ☐

3   A ☐   B ☐   C ☐

4
Dave Ford,
Flat A
Ground floor,
Churchill Court

Dave Ford,
Flat A
4th floor,
Churchill Court

Dave Ford,
Flat A
1st floor,
Churchill Court

A ☐   B ☐   C ☐

6 Extension *Time to talk*

a Martin is having a conversation with a new friend. Read what he says.

MARTIN:
• How old are you?
• Where do you live?
• Do you live in a flat?
• Have you got your own room?
• What are your neighbours like?

🔊 Now listen to the conversation.

b Read Martin's sentences again. Then imagine he's talking to you. Think about the answers you want to make.

c 🔊 Close your book, listen to the sentences and respond.

Unit 2   9

1 one / ones G→ 31

Write the second sentence in a more natural way.
Use *one/ones*.

1 These jeans are very expensive. I'd like some cheaper jeans.

I'd like _some cheaper ones_ .

2 You can't take photos with this mobile. I want a mobile with a camera.

I want _____ .

3 A: Do you want an ice cream?
   B: Yes, I'd like a chocolate ice cream.

Yes, I'd like _____ .

4 I didn't buy a shirt. I couldn't find a nice shirt.

I couldn't find _____ .

5 This box isn't very big. Have you got any bigger boxes?

Have you got _____ ?

2 the one / ones + relative pronoun G→ 30, 31

Read about Martha and answer the questions. Use *the one/ones* + *who, that* or *which*.

Martha lives in Marston Street. Marston Street goes from London Road into the town centre.

Martha lives at number 36. She knows Anne and Peter. They live next door, at number 38, but she's never met her other neighbours, Mr and Mrs Collins. They live at number 34.

There are three shops in the street. One shop sells shoes, another sells flowers and the third sells camping equipment.

Martha's got two brothers. One brother's at university, and the other owns the shoe shop in Marston Street. He earns a lot of money.

1 Which street is Marston Street?

It's _the one that goes from London Road into the town_

centre.

2 Does Martha know all her neighbours?

No, she doesn't know _____ number 34.

3 Who are Anne and Peter?

They're _____ .

4 Yesterday Martha bought a new sleeping bag. Which shop did she go to?

She went _____ .

5 Which of Martha's brothers has got a good job?

The _____ .

3 Key expressions
Asking for clarification

Look at the picture and complete the dialogue. Use the words in the box.

> Is he the one who
> Which one do you mean
> Do you mean the one that
> Is he the one with

A: These are my friends. That's Maria.

B: ¹_____

_____ ?

A: The one with the tennis racket.
   Then there's George, the tall one.

B: ²_____

_____ 's laughing?

A: No, I don't. That isn't George.

B: ³_____

_____ sunglasses?

A: Yes, that's George. And that's Paul.

B: ⁴_____

_____ 's playing the

guitar?

A: Yes, that's right.

4 Reading *Neighbours*

Read the text. Then read the questions and circle the right answer: a, b, c or d.

A recent survey found that most people in Britain think that good neighbours are very important. One out of five people share their family problems with their neighbours and they often ask them for advice.

We all like the idea of having good neighbours but, in reality, we don't always have a good relationship with them. Many families want to move because they hate the people who live next door.

The main cause of the problem is noise: stereos and televisions that are too loud, vacuum cleaners at two o'clock in the morning, electric drills, families that have arguments all the time. If your neighbours are noisy, particularly the ones who live in the flat above you, life can be very unpleasant.

Outside in the street, there's another problem: neighbours often argue about parking places. 'Move your car! You've parked in my place.' 'I was here before you. You don't own the street, you know!' They shout and sometimes they even fight.

25% of people in the survey said they never speak to their neighbours. A man who recently sold his flat in North London said he spoke to his neighbours for the first time on the day he was leaving. The first thing he said to them, after ten years, was 'Goodbye'!

1 What do most people in Britain say?
  a We share our problems with our neighbours.
  b We always get on well with our neighbours.
  c We ask our neighbours for advice.
  d We would like to have good neighbours.

2 According to the text, which of these sentences is true?
  a Most people hate their neighbours.
  b 20% of people have got neighbours who are good friends.
  c People who live in flats want to move.
  d Neighbours are always difficult.

3 Which are the most difficult neighbours?
  a The ones that make a lot of noise.
  b The ones who listen to music.
  c The ones who park their cars in the street.
  d The ones that like watching television.

4 A man who lived in a flat in North London
  a sold his flat when his neighbours left.
  b didn't speak to his neighbours for ten years.
  c spoke to his neighbours for the first time on the day they were leaving.
  d said goodbye to his neighbours ten years ago.

5 Extension *What are they talking about?*

Can you say what these people are talking about?

1 I like the blue ones with the white belt. ....

2 Let's watch the one about whales. ....

3 I'm reading a good one about space travel at the moment. ....

4 I'll send one to Alex now. Where's my mobile? ....

5 We had a meal at the one in Church Street yesterday. ....

'Friendship questionnaire':
Vocabulary check

1 Look at the words in the box. Find three words to match the stress pattern of *honesty*.

honesty	sense of humour	less
respect	quality	chat	secretive
sociable	control	get on well

●●● ___honesty___ _____

_____ _____

2 Complete the sentences. Use the words in the box in Exercise 1.

1 There was ice on the road, so the driver couldn't _____ the car and it hit a tree.

2 I often _____ to my friends on my mobile before I go to bed.

3 My boyfriend isn't very _____ . He hates going to parties.

4 I have my lunch in the canteen because it's _____ expensive than the café.

5 Patience is an important _____ for a teacher!

6 I can never believe what Amy says. She doesn't know what _____ means.

7 No one knows what Paul really thinks. He's a very _____ person.

8 A _____ is important. We mustn't be serious all the time!

9 Nadia and Clare spend a lot of time together. They _____ with each other.

10 Roger doesn't _____ other people. He's often rude and he never listens to other people's opinions.

3 Translate these sentences into your language.

1 A: Is there a train which goes to London this evening?
  B: Yes, there's one that leaves at half past seven.

_____

_____

_____

2 A: Dave's flat is the one with a balcony, on the third floor.
  B: Do you mean the one that's got a red door?

_____

_____

_____

3 A: Do you know Mr and Mrs Welch?
  B: Are they the ones who own the café?

_____

_____

_____

4 A: Where's Richard?
  B: He's working at the supermarket. He works there every Saturday morning.

_____

_____

_____

5 Honesty and thoughtfulness are two very important qualities.

_____

_____

6 I like people who respect my opinions.

_____

_____

Unit 2 Learning diary

Date _____

Now I know how to:

	Easy	Not bad	Difficult
describe where people live, using the present simple.	☐	☐	☐

Where _____ Helen live? She _____ in a block of flats. Her flat's on the first floor, so she _____ usually take the lift.

use relative clauses.	☐	☐	☐

A newsagent's is a shop that _____ newspapers and magazines.

Your neighbours are the people _____ next door to you.

A koala is an animal _____ in Australia.

use *one/ones*.	☐	☐	☐

I'd like three bottles, a large _____ and two small _____ .

I like both flats, but I prefer the _____ that's got a balcony.

ask for clarification.	☐	☐	☐

The Taylors? _____ mean the people who live on the third floor?

_____ Winston the one who plays the trumpet?

Can you see that boy over there? _____ one do you mean?

express my opinions about friendships.	☐	☐	☐

KEY WORDS
Flats and houses

block of flats _____

_____

_____

_____

_____

_____

WORD WORK
Personal qualities

ADJECTIVE

selfish _____

_____

_____

_____

_____

_____

NOUN

selfishness _____

_____

_____

_____

_____

_____

3 All in the mind

1 Past simple and past continuous (G) → 8

Complete the conversation. Choose from the list (a–i).

ANNIE: ¹ _d_ a strange experience yesterday.

TOM: What happened?

ANNIE: Well, while ² .... my lunch in the café, I smelt cigarette smoke. And I suddenly thought about my flat.

TOM: What about the other people in the cafe? ³ .... ?

ANNIE: No, you can't smoke in the café.

TOM: ⁴ .... ?

ANNIE: I went home immediately. When I arrived, I saw a man outside my flat.

TOM: What was he doing?

ANNIE: ⁵ .... to open the door.

TOM: ⁶ .... when he saw you?

ANNIE: He ran away. And it was really weird. ⁷ .... a cigarette.

TOM: Amazing. Perhaps you're telepathic!

a	What did he do	f	He tried
b	What did you do	g	I was having
c	He was trying	h	Were they
~~d~~	~~I had~~		smoking
e	He was smoking	i	He smoked

2 Listening *What were they doing?*

Listen to the sounds and voices. Then choose the right words and write complete sentences.

1 When she
- was walking to school,
- went to school,   a dog
- was going to school,

- was attacking her.
- attacked her.
- ran away from her.

When she .... , a dog ....

2 Someone
- was coming to the flat
- came to the flat   when he
- spoke to him

- had a shower.
- was having a shower.
- was coming out of the shower.

Someone .... when he ....

3 While they
- were having dinner,
- were cooking dinner,   they
- had dinner,

- made a weird noise.
- were hearing strange noises.
- heard a strange noise.

While they .... , they ....

4 They
- played football
- didn't stop playing   when the ball
- were playing football

- was hitting the window.
- hit the window.
- was breaking the window.

They .... when the ball ....

5 When she
- looked for her passport,
- was looking for the photo,   she
- was looking for her passport,

- was at primary school.
- found an old photo.
- found her passport.

When she .... , she ....

3 Past simple and past continuous: negative forms and questions

G ➤ 8

a Complete these sentences. Use the past simple or past continuous. You'll sometimes need to use the negative form of the verb.

1 My dad _wasn't watching_ (watch) the road when he _____hit_____ (hit) the car in front of him.

2 I _____ (play) volleyball for the school team yesterday, but we _____ _____ (win).

3 We _____ (miss) the last bus, so we _____ (get) home until 2 am.

4 Tim and Fran _____ (go) surfing because it was late and it _____ _____ (get) dark.

5 The teacher suddenly _____ (get) angry because we _____ _____ (listen) to her.

b Write two questions for each sentence.

1 Jack found an old key while he was looking for his camera.

What _was Jack doing?_

What _did he find?_

2 Leo met Gemma when he was going to the bus stop.

Who _____ ?

Where _____ ?

3 While they were staying in Rome, Helen and Amy lost their passports.

Where _____ ?

What _____ ?

4 While she was watching TV in the living room, Sonia smelt smoke.

What _____ ?

What _____ ?

4 Key expressions *Expressing surprise*

Complete the dialogue. Use all the expressions (a–e) in the box.

a	How weird!	d	Really?
b	You're joking!	e	What a coincidence!
c	That's strange		

LIAM: I got an email from Lucy yesterday.

CHLOE: ¹........ She's on holiday in France, isn't she?

LIAM: Yes, and she met the French prime minister's son on the beach.

CHLOE: ²........

LIAM: No, I'm not. It's true. He was sitting next to her. He had a green surfboard, exactly the same as hers.

CHLOE: ³........

LIAM: I know. So they started a conversation, but Lucy didn't say much.

CHLOE: ⁴........ , because she speaks French well.

LIAM: I know, but she was really nervous. And she said she had a strange dream last night. She was surfing with the French prime minister's son. And they were going through the Channel Tunnel!

CHLOE: ⁵........

5 Extension *How weird!*

Think of some weird situations and write sentences like these in your notebook.

While I was cleaning my teeth, the toothbrush jumped out of my hand and flew out of the window.

When I arrived at school, everyone was wearing red T-shirts and blue shorts.

When I spoke to Claire, she fell on the floor and started to laugh.

1 Key vocabulary *Fears and fantasies*

Complete the sentences. Use the words in the box.

have nightmares   worry about   pretend   feel nervous
frighten   believe in   dream about   make up

1 I don't _____ aliens. I don't think they exist.

2 I always _____ when I go in a lift.

3 When I _____ funny things, I often laugh in my sleep.

4 When I play with my little brother, I sometimes _____ I'm Superman.

5 Use your imagination! _____ a story about an exciting adventure.

6 You're so pessimistic. You always _____ the future.

7 When I see a scary film, I often _____ when I go to sleep.

8 You _____ me when you get angry.

2 *used to*: affirmative form → 9

Read the sentences and say what Alice's grandfather used to do in the past. Use the verbs in the box.

get   ~~play~~   listen to   go camping   ride
be interested in

Alice is looking at things in her grandfather's house. Her grandfather is very old now and he spends most of his time in bed.

1 Alice found three tennis balls and an old racket.

   Her grandfather used to play tennis.

2 There were some binoculars and lots of books about birds.

   He _____ .

3 Alice found an old bike.

   He _____ .

4 There was an old tent with holes in it.

   He _____ .

5 There were a lot of old letters from someone in Australia.

   He _____ .

6 There was a collection of old records of American jazz music.

   He _____ .

3 *used to*: negative forms 9

Mr and Mrs Talbot have suddenly changed. They're doing a lot of new things that they didn't do before. Write sentences using *didn't use to* and *never used to*.

1 *They didn't use to go jogging.*

2 Mrs Talbot _____ a bike.

3 They never _____ the gym.

4 Mr Talbot _____ modern clothes.

5 Mrs Talbot _____ a computer.

4 *used to*: questions G➤ 9

Put the words in the right order and make B's questions.

1 A: This Russian dictionary used to belong to my
    great grandmother.
   B: she / speak / use / Russian / to / did ?

   ....

2 A: People used to think I was crazy.
   B: use / did / do / you / to / what ?

   ....

3 A: My mum used to love hip-hop.
   B: like / to / groups / she / use / which / did ?

   ....

4 A: I used to live in the USA.
   B: accent / speak / American / an / did / to /
    use / you / with ?

   ....

5 Reading *He was very lucky!*

Read the text, then look at the sentences and say who's speaking.

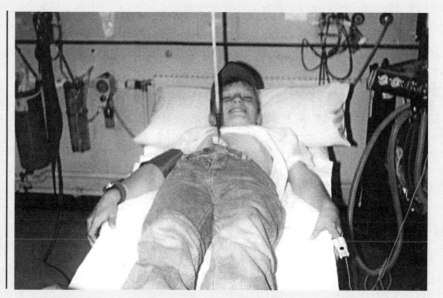

Nat Spink will never forget the day when he went to hospital with a 90 cm arrow in his stomach. He's still got the photo that was in the local newspaper. In the photo he was lying on a hospital bed and he was feeling a bit scared, but he gave the photographer a big smile!

Nat used to play with his friends in the park. They never used to think that their games were dangerous and Nat's mother didn't use to worry about him. Then, one day, when Nat was 12, his best friend made a bow and arrow. The arrow was a piece of bamboo with a long nail at the end. They went into the park with some other boys. Nat's friend tried the bow and arrow. The other boys were standing several metres away from him and they all moved, except Nat. The arrow hit him in the stomach. Nat said later that he saw the arrow coming towards him. He knew it was going to hit him, but he didn't have time to move.

Someone called an ambulance and Nat was taken to hospital. Doctors cut the bamboo, then they took out the nail. 'Fortunately, the injury wasn't too serious,' they said, 'but he was very, very lucky.'

1 'We don't take arrows out of people every day!'   ....

2 'I never used to worry about Nat when he was playing outside.' ....

3 'I wasn't trying to hit Nat. It was an accident.'   ....

4 'We moved when we saw the arrow coming.'   ....

5 'I smiled, but I was feeling nervous.'   ....

6 Extension *Other people's fears*

Think about your friends and family and write sentences about their fears in your notebook.

My friend Giorgio feels nervous when he flies in a plane.
My grandmother worries about her health.

'The importance of dreams': Vocabulary check

1 Look at the words in the box. Can you find one adverb?

come true	properly	deep	breathing	active
fear	freedom	mind	as	soldier	guard	cover

....

2 Match 1–9 with a–i and make complete sentences.

1 I can't walk properly
2 I have a lot of wonderful dreams,
3 I'd like to have Superman's body
4 I love the feeling of freedom
5 At Buckingham Palace, tourists take photos of the soldiers
6 As I climbed up the hill,
7 Last winter the snow was very deep
8 My grandmother's a very active person and
9 I'm scared of getting old. In fact,

a and Einstein's mind.
b that's my greatest fear.
c because these shoes are too small.
d and it nearly covered our car.
e she still plays tennis and goes jogging.
f my breathing got faster.
g when the school holidays begin.
h but they never come true.
i who guard the entrance.

1 .... 2 .... 3 .... 4 .... 5 .... 6 .... 7 .... 8 .... 9 ....

3 Translate these sentences into your language.

1 What was Oliver doing when you saw him?

....
....
....

2 A: While Jill was having her breakfast this morning, she heard her name on the radio.
   B: Really?

....
....
....

3 A: When I was in bed last night, the bed suddenly moved! I wasn't dreaming.
   B: How weird! What did you do?

....
....
....
....

4 People didn't use to come to this beach. It used to be quiet in summer, but now it's full of tourists.

....
....
....
....

5 Did you use to be frightened of dogs when you were little?

....
....
....

6 At first, Colin felt OK in the boat, but then the weather changed and he started to feel nervous.

....
....
....

Unit 3 Learning diary

Date _____

Now I know how to:

	Easy	Not bad	Difficult

- describe events in the past, using the past simple and the past continuous. ☐ ☐ ☐

  When she saw John on the beach, he _____ shorts and a T-shirt.

  While they were playing football, the ball _____ Simon in the face.

  When I was _____ to school this morning, I _____ .

- express surprise. ☐ ☐ ☐

  When Kelly and Joanna arrived at the party, they were both wearing the same dress.

  _____ ?   What _____ !

  I'm going to be on television tomorrow.   You _____ !

- talk about fears and fantasies. ☐ ☐ ☐

  I always feel nervous when _____ .

  I often dream about _____ .

- talk about regular past activities using *used to*. ☐ ☐ ☐

  Tim _____ have piano lessons, but he doesn't play the piano now.

  Anne _____ like tomatoes, but she often eats them now.

  I used to _____ .

  I didn't use to _____ .

- describe a dream. ☐ ☐ ☐

KEY WORDS

Fears and fantasies

have nightmares	= _____ *(in my language)*
make up stories	= _____
frighten	= _____
pretend	= _____
feel nervous	= _____
worry about something	= _____
dream about something	= _____
believe in something	= _____

WORD WORK

Link words

when _____

as _____

at first _____

_____

_____

4 Journeys

1 Obligations: *must, mustn't* and *have to* G→ 16, 17

Complete these sentences about driving in Britain. Use <u>one</u> word in each space.

1 If you drive a car in Britain, you ..... *must* ..... remember these rules.

2 You .... to drive on the left.

3 You and your passengers .... wear seatbelts.

4 You .... use a mobile phone while you're driving.

5 You .... to be able to understand British road signs.

6 You .... drive too close to the car in front.

2 *have to*: questions G→ 16

Complete the questions using the right form of *have to*.

1 A: You must clean your room.

   B: *Do I have to* do it now?

2 A: My sister works in a hotel.

   B: .... work at the weekend?

3 A: Tourists can spend two weeks in the Sahara desert.

   B: .... sleep in tents?

4 A: Let's go to the sports centre.

   B: .... pay?

5 A: Jack's got a job at a restaurant.

   B: What .... do?

6 A: Visitors to the factory have to wear special clothes.

   B: Why .... do that?

3 *mustn't / don't have to* G→ 17

Match the pictures (1–6) with the sentences (a–f).

a He mustn't work this afternoon.

b You mustn't go up the stairs.

c He doesn't have to work this afternoon.

d You mustn't take the car.

e You don't have to go up the stairs.

f You don't have to take the car.

1 .... 2 .... 3 .... 4 .... 5 .... 6 ....

4 Comparatives (G) ➔ 32

Write sentences to show the difference between these things. Use the comparative form of the adjectives in the box.

| high | easy | ~~short~~ | comfortable | big | good |

1 From London, a flight to Paris / a flight to Madrid

From London, a flight to Paris is shorter than a flight to Madrid.

2 In an exam, $\frac{16}{20}$ / 75%

3 A town / a village

4 Most language students think that English / Chinese

5 A mountain / a hill

6 A five-star hotel / a two-star hotel

5 Key expressions *Making travel arrangements*

Match what the customer says (1–5) with the travel agent's replies (a–e).

1 I'd like to book a ticket to London, please.

2 How far is it to London from here?

3 How long does it take to get there?

4 It takes me half an hour to get from my flat to the coach station.

5 How can I get from the coach station in London to the Science Museum?

a About two hours by coach.

b When do you want to leave?

c Get the tube. It's quicker than the bus.

d About 140 kilometres.

e Well, don't be late. The coach always leaves on time.

1 .... 2 .... 3 .... 4 .... 5 ....

6 Listening *The London Marathon*

🔊 Listen to the description of the London Marathon. Then answer the questions. Circle the right answer: a, b or c.

1 How many people run in the London Marathon?
   a About 40.
   b About 40,000.
   c About 4,000.

2 How long is a marathon?
   a Four days.
   b Just over two hours.
   c 42 kilometres.

3 Who runs in the London Marathon?
   a Lots of ordinary people.
   b Only professional sports people.
   c Only people who wear funny clothes.

4 What happened a few years ago?
   a Two runners got married after the race.
   b Two runners had their wedding before the race.
   c Two runners got married while they were doing the race.

5 How long did it take Lloyd Scott to complete the race?
   a 5 hours, 29 minutes and 46 seconds.
   b 5 days, 8 hours, 29 minutes and 46 seconds.
   c 5 days, 18 hours, 46 minutes and 29 seconds.

7 Extension *Time to talk*

a Jessie is having a conversation with a new friend. Read what she says.

JESSIE:
   • How far is it to school from your house?
   • How do you get to school?
   • How long does it take?
   • Do you go into town at the weekend?
   • Well, shall we look round the shops on Saturday morning?

🔊 Now listen to the conversation.

b Read Jessie's sentences again. Then imagine she's talking to you. Think about the answers you want to make.

c 🔊 Close your book, listen to the sentences and respond.

1 Key vocabulary *On the road*

Complete the crossword.

Across

1 When you're on the road, you mustn't go faster than this.

7 You wear this to protect your head.

8 Andy's got one. It's a Harley-Davidson.

9 The traffic goes round in a circle here.

Down

2 If you don't visit this place, your car won't go far.

3 It's bigger than a car, but it doesn't carry passengers.

4 If they're red, you have to stop here.

5 It's faster than a bicycle, but it isn't as powerful as '8 across'.

6 '8 across' has got two of these.

2 The passive (G) → 20

Complete the sentences using the present simple passive or the past simple passive.

1 Today, more than 2,000 languages __are spoken__ (*speak*) in Africa.

2 A violin .... (*make*) from about 70 different pieces of wood.

3 In the USA, 22 kilograms of chocolate .... (*eat*) every second.

4 Wild tigers .... (*not find*) in North America, but about 7,000 tigers .... (*keep*) as pets in the USA.

5 $11,000,000,000 .... (*spend*) on pet food every year.

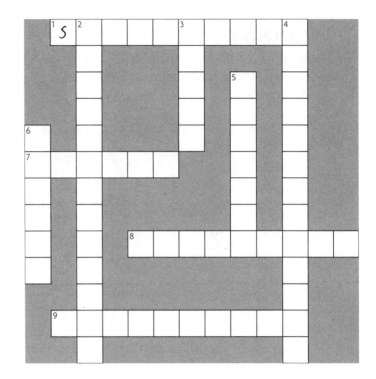

6 The Greek poet Aeschylus .... (*kill*) by a tortoise. It hit him on the head when it .... (*drop*) by a bird.

7 The game of hockey .... first .... (*play*) in Egypt over 4,000 years ago.

8 The planet Pluto .... (*not discover*) until 1930.

3 The passive (G) → 20

Write the sentences in a different way. Use the present simple passive or the past simple passive.

1 Someone wrote this song in the 1960s.

This song was written in the 1960s.

2 Someone makes these scooters in Italy.

....

3 Someone stole my father's motorbike yesterday.

....

4 They don't grow tea in Britain.

....

5 The Romans didn't invent the wheel.

....

6 People spend a lot of money on clothes.

....

4 Reading *March of the Penguins*

Read the text about emperor penguins. Then look at the sentences (1–8) and write *T* (true) or *F* (false).

The film *March of the Penguins* tells the story of one of the most incredible journeys in the world. Every year in April, at the beginning of the Antarctic winter, thousands of emperor penguins walk 100 km from the sea to the place where their young are born. They travel across the ice at 1.5 kph, walking day and night. They cross a region where no other wild creature can survive. The temperature is often –40° C and there are icy winds of 160 kph.

At the end of their long journey, the penguins choose their partners, and in May the female produces one egg. Then she goes back to the sea to eat, and the male looks after the egg. For two months he doesn't eat, and he loses 50% of his weight. Finally, the baby penguin is born and the female returns. The male then walks back to the sea to find food. As the baby gets older, both parents bring food for it, and in December it's ready to survive on its own.

The film was made by the French film director, Luc Jacquet, and his two cameramen. They spent over a year following the penguins. The film was first shown in France, then an English version was made. No one is sure why a documentary film about penguins was so successful, but it was a big hit all over the world.

1 The penguins' young are born near the sea. ....

2 During their journey, the penguins walk 24 hours a day. ....

3 Only one egg is produced by the female. ....

4 The eggs are guarded by the females for most of the time. ....

5 During the Antarctic winter the penguins make the journey to and from the sea several times. ....

6 After about a month the young can survive on their own. ....

7 The film wasn't made for French-speaking countries. ....

8 Documentary films aren't usually as successful as *March of the Penguins*. ....

5 Extension *What is it?*

Read these clues and guess what this is.

The [?] that is eaten today was probably invented in the 16th century in southern Italy. It's a sort of bread that is covered with cheese, tomatoes, olives, seafood or ham, and then it's cooked in a hot oven. Now it's eaten all over the world in restaurants and cafés, and it's sold in supermarkets. It wasn't invented in Pisa!

....

Write some clues for something else. Then ask a friend if he/she can guess what it is.

'A very long bike ride':
Vocabulary check

1 Look at the words in the box. Can you find a noun that has got two meanings?

on her way to	safely	plan	in the end	last	
bank	chase	run out of	backpacker	fall off	

....

2 Write the underlined words in a different way. Use the words in the box in Exercise 1.

1 Be careful! Don't go so fast. You might not stay on your bike.

----

2 When Paula saw the dog, she ran away. Luckily, the dog didn't run after her.

----

3 Kirsty's walking along the street. She's carrying a sports bag. She's going to the sports centre.

----

4 Tara's fine. She's arrived with no problem.

----

5 Jenny and Helen are going to London next weekend. They've decided to go round the shops in Oxford Street.

----

6 I couldn't decide what to do last night. Finally, I decided to go to bed.

----

7 This weather's awful. They say it'll continue until Thursday.

----

8 He jumped into the river and swam to the other side.

----

9 I don't think we'll get home. We're going to use all our petrol before we get there.

----

10 When I was travelling in Africa, I met another boy with a rucksack on the road to Nairobi.

----

3 Translate these sentences into your language.

1 A: How long does it take to get to the station?
   B: Only about five minutes. We don't have to hurry.

----

2 In Britain, if you ride a motorbike, you have to wear a helmet.

----

3 You mustn't forget to book a seat on the train.

----

4 A: How do you get to the park?
   B: Go down South Street to the traffic lights. Turn left and go across the square. You'll see the park in front of you.

----

5 Let's go to the travel agent's in King Street. It's nearer than the one in Mill Road.

----

6 Football and rugby are played all over the world, but the games were both invented by the English.

Unit 4 Learning diary

Date _____

Now I know how to:

	Easy	Not bad	Difficult

- talk about obligations. ☐ ☐ ☐

  We must hurry. We have to be at the airport at 10 o'clock. We _____ be late.

  At home, I have to _____ .

  I like the holidays, because I don't have to _____ .

- compare things. ☐ ☐ ☐

  The train is expensive. Go by bus. It's _____ .

  I think _____ is more _____ than _____ .

- make travel arrangements. ☐ ☐ ☐

  _____ does it take to get to London?   It takes about an hour.

  How _____ is it?   It's about forty kilometres.

  I'd like to _____ a ticket to Rome, please.

  How can I _____ the station from here?

- talk about things that are done or were done. ☐ ☐ ☐

  Harley-Davidson motorbikes _____ made in America.

  I didn't go to the party because I _____ invited.

  This white suit _____ by Elvis Presley in the 1960s.

- write a journal about a trip. ☐ ☐ ☐

KEY WORDS

On the road

lorry _____

_____

_____

_____

_____

_____

_____

_____

WORD WORK

Prepositions of movement

go	_____	a hill	↑
go	_____	a hill	↓
walk	_____	a path	→
go	_____	a room	⊕→
swim	_____	a lake	⊖→
go	_____	a lake	⟲→
climb	_____	a window	⊖→
go	_____	A to B	Ⓐ→Ⓑ

In the news

1 Key vocabulary *Topics in the news*

Complete the names of these newspaper topics.

- **T _ e _ _ _ _ r _ _ m _ n _**
  The Arctic ice is melting more quickly.

- **W _ _ a _ _ _ e _ c _**
  Britain needs more soldiers.

- **_ _ _ l t _**
  Students ask for healthier food at school!

- **F _ m _ _ s _ e _ p _ e**
  Jude Law's new film is a huge hit.

- **_ _ l _ _ i _ s**
  The government's problems are getting worse.

- **_ h _ _ e _ t _ _ r**
  The weekend will be warm and sunny.

- **C _ _ m _**
  3,000 cars are stolen in London every year.

- **_ _ o _ t**
  Can England win the World Cup?

2 Present perfect: affirmative (G)→ 3

Complete the sentences. Use the affirmative form of the present perfect with the verbs in the box.

| bite | swim | mend | forget | paint | fall off |

1 Oh no! He ....
  his horse.

2 Look! She ....
  a bird.

3 I ....

4 That dog ....
  my arm.

5 She ....
  50 km.

6 They ....
  the washing machine.

3 Present perfect: negative G→ 3

Write a second sentence each time. Use the negative form of the present perfect.

1 I'm not ready. (*I / finish / my breakfast*) _I haven't finished my breakfast._

2 I had a horrible dream last night. (*But it / come true*) ....

3 I don't know where Tom is. (*He / phone*) ....

4 Your arm's OK. (*You / break / it*) ....

5 I'm not going to their party. (*They / invite / me*) ....

4 Present perfect: questions and short answers G→ 3

Put the words in the right order and make questions. Then answer the questions.

1 to / Danny / written / Callum / recently / has ?

Has Danny written to Callum recently?   No, _he hasn't_ .

2 busy / been / Danny / has ?

....   Yes, ...

3 parents / have / gone / Danny's / France / to ?

....   No, ...

4 Lorina / baby / has / another / had ?

....   Yes, ...

5 Present perfect + *just* G→ 4

Write these sentences in a different way. Use the present perfect with *just*.

1 The train left two minutes ago. _The train has just left._

2 My cousin had a baby a couple of days ago. ....

3 Our neighbours went to Australia this morning. ....

4 The match started a few minutes ago. ....

5 I heard the news about Rob on my way home this evening. ....

6 *been* and *gone* G→ 7

Brian's waiting for his friends Alison and Tim. Complete the conversation using *been* or *gone*.

BRIAN: Alison! You're late. Where have you [1] _been_ ?

ALISON: Sorry. I've [2] .... to the airport. My dad's [3] .... to Japan. I went to the airport with him to say goodbye.

BRIAN: Is Tim coming?

ALISON: No, he's at home. He's [4] .... to the dentist, and now he isn't feeling very well, so he's

[5] .... to bed.

7 Extension *Good news!*

In your notebook, write at least three pieces of news you would like to hear.

All the wars in the world have stopped. They've decided to give students longer holidays.

1 Present perfect with *already* and *yet* G→ 4

Complete B's replies. Use the verbs in the present perfect with *already* or *yet*.

1 A: There's a good film at the Odeon cinema this week.

B: I *'ve already seen it* . (*see/it*) It was really funny.

2 A: I must say goodbye to the Kellys before they leave.

B: You're too late. They .... (*leave*)

3 A: Is Colin going to come with us tonight?

B: He isn't sure. He .... (*not decide*)

4 A: Is everyone here?

B: What about Jamie? .... he .... ? (*arrive*)

5 A: I think I'll take these shoes back to the shop.

B: You can't do that. You .... them. (*wear*)

6 A: Where's Olivia?

B: I don't know. She .... (*not come home*)

2 Present perfect and past simple G→ 3

Circle the right reply: a or b.

1 What was the concert like last night?
   a I don't know. I haven't been.
   b I don't know. I didn't go.

2 I love Italian food.
   a Me too. Have you been to Italy?
   b Me too. Did you go to Italy?

3 Vicky looks very upset.
   a Perhaps she's had some bad news.
   b Perhaps she had some bad news.

4 I saw Beth at the station this morning.
   a Have you spoken to her?
   b Did you speak to her?

5 I can't find my mobile phone.
   a I hope you didn't lose it.
   b I hope you haven't lost it.

6 Have you ever met Helen's French pen friend?
   a Yes, she came to my birthday party.
   b Yes, she's come to my birthday party.

3 Key expressions *Offers and suggestions*

Complete the conversation. Use the words in the list (a–h).

DAD: ¹........ turn off the computer?

TINA: No, don't do that. I haven't finished my homework yet. We have to write an essay about an interesting inventor.

DAD: ²........ help you if you like. I'm not busy.

TINA: ³........ , thanks. I'll do it. But I'm not interested in inventors.

DAD: ⁴........ write about Leonardo da Vinci?

TINA: I don't know anything about him.

DAD: Well, ⁵........ look on the Internet.

TINA: But it's so boring! ⁶........ you write a note to my teacher? You ⁷........ tell him I haven't done the essay because I've been ill.

DAD: ⁸........ Come on! It's getting late.

TINA: Oh, all right then. How do you spell 'Leonardo'?

a	I could
b	No, it's all right
c	Why don't you
d	could
e	Shall I
f	No, I can't do that.
g	Why don't
h	you could

4 Listening *Ambitions*

🎙 Listen to the description of John Goddard and his list of achievements.

a Answer these questions.

1 How many things did John write on his list? .... 2 How many things has he already done? ....

b Listen again and look at the pictures. Write ✓ for the things that John has already done and ✗ for the things that he hasn't done yet.

Mount Everest

The North Pole

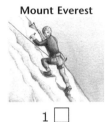    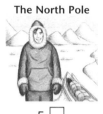 

1 ☐   2 ☐   3 ☐   4 ☐   5 ☐   6 ☐

5 Reading *Hamster power*

Read the text about Peter Ash. Then complete the sentences (1–8) using words from the text.

The modern world needs more and more energy. Can you imagine our world without electricity? No computers, no television, no telephones, no Internet!

We've used oil, gas, coal and nuclear power to create the energy we need. Now, thanks to modern technology, we're using the power of the wind and the sea as well. But will the world have enough energy in twenty years' time? Scientists and politicians are trying to find answers to one of the biggest problems in the world today.

16-year-old Peter Ash from Somerset in southwest England has thought about the problem too. Peter was studying electronics at school and he had to do a project about electricity. One day he was watching his pet hamster, called Elvis. Elvis was playing on the wheel in his cage. As the hamster ran inside the wheel, the wheel went faster and faster. Peter suddenly had an idea for his project. He built a simple machine and attached it to the wheel. He used Elvis's energy to create electricity, and he found there was enough electricity to charge his mobile phone. When Elvis played on his wheel for two minutes, Peter got 30 minutes' 'talk time' on his mobile.

Perhaps Peter hasn't saved the world, but he passed his electronics exam!

1 A computer won't work if there isn't any ....

2 Oil, gas, coal and nuclear power are all forms of ....

3 We can use the .... of the sea as well.

4 One of Peter Ash's school subjects was ....

5 Peter's .... gave him an idea for his project.

6 Elvis used his .... to get some exercise.

7 Peter made a .... which changed Elvis's energy into electricity.

8 Peter used his invention to make electricity for his ....

6 Extension *Puzzle*

Look again at the text about Elvis the hamster in Exercise 5. Then answer this question.

Imagine you've got Peter's machine and a hamster that plays on its wheel for four hours a day. In one day, how many people will be able to get 30 minutes' talk time on their mobile phones?

....

'Yellowstone's hot secret': Vocabulary check

1 Look at the words in the box. Can you find two words that describe dangerous events?

| ash | earthquake | geyser | fascinated | over | movement | giant | eruption | increase | alive |

....

2 These sentences are wrong! ~~Cross out~~ the wrong word and find the right word in the box in Exercise 1.

1   When a volcano explodes, it sends clouds of fish into the air.   ....

2   This spider's moving. Look! It's still dead.   ....

3   If there are more cars on the road, the number of accidents will fall.   ....

4   A jumper is a column of hot water that comes out of the ground.   ....

5   Hey! Don't walk under those flowers. I've just planted them.   ....

6   It was a very interesting film and the children were all bored.   ....

7   When a volcano explodes, the event is called 'a volcanic exhibition'.   ....

8   When there's an accident, the ground moves.   ....

9   The anaconda is a small snake.   ....

10   Scientists who study earthquakes use machines that can
record the smallest song.   ....

3 Translate these sentences into your language.

1   I've just seen the news on TV. There's been an
earthquake in Italy.

....

....

....

2   A: Where has Meg gone?
B: She's gone to Turkey. She's already been to
France and Greece this year.

....

....

....

3   A: What have you done with the old vacuum
cleaner?
B: I've thrown it away.

....

....

....

4   A: Have you been to the cinema recently?
B: Yes, I went on Saturday, but it was such an awful
film that I left before the end.

....

....

....

5   A: Have you contacted Tim?
B: Yes, I sent him an email last week, but he hasn't
replied yet.

....

....

....

6   A: I've got nothing to do this morning.
B: Why don't you phone a friend? Or you could go to
the leisure centre.

....

....

....

Unit 5 Learning diary

Date _____

Now I know how to:

	Easy	Not bad	Difficult

- talk about things that have happened recently. ☐ ☐ ☐

  Our neighbours _____ bought a new car.

  I _____ just _____ a great film.

  I've _____ .

- use *yet* and *already* with the present perfect. ☐ ☐ ☐

  I'm looking for my maths book. I _____ found it yet.

  Has the match started _____ ?

  Is Sally there?   No, she's _____ left.

  I've already _____ .   I haven't _____ yet.

- use *been* and *gone*. ☐ ☐ ☐

  Hi, Leo. Where have you _____ ?

  Where's Nadia?   She's _____ to the shops.

- ask for or give more details after a sentence in the present perfect. ☐ ☐ ☐

  I've just had a text message from Joe.   What _____ he say?

  Have you seen Alan?   Yes, I _____ him this morning on the bus.

- make offers and suggestions. ☐ ☐ ☐

  _____ I do the shopping?

  We've got nothing to do.   _____ you play cards? Or you

  could _____ .

- write some news for a school newsletter. ☐ ☐ ☐

KEY WORDS

Topics in the news

war and peace _____   _____

_____   _____

_____   _____

WORD WORK

so + adjective / *such a, an* + adjective + noun

The book was so long that I got bored.

It was _____ a long book that I got bored.

My headache was so bad that I went to bed.

I had _____

_____

6 Attachments

1 How long + present perfect

For each sentence, make a question using *How long* + present perfect.

1 Mr and Mrs Pringle have got a parrot called Frank.

   How long have they had it?

2 Andy has got a Harley-Davidson motorbike.

   .... it?

3 Winston is in South Africa at the moment.

   .... there?

4 Mr and Mrs Gray know the manager of the Liverpool football team.

   .... him?

5 Beth works for a local radio station.

   .... there?

6 I live in a flat on the eighth floor.

   .... there?

2 *for* and *since* Ⓖ➔ 5

Complete the sentences. Use *for* or *since*.

1 I haven't seen my cousin Nella ......*since*...... I was ten.

2 Laura has been ill .... three days now.

3 We haven't had a camping holiday .... a long time.

4 There haven't been any trains .... Monday.

5 It hasn't rained .... a fortnight.

6 My gran has lived in the same house .... she was born.

3 Present perfect + *for* and *since* Ⓖ➔ 5

Write the sentences in a different way. Use the present perfect (affirmative or negative) with *for* or *since*.

1 Yuri went to hospital when he had the accident, and he's still there.

   (*be*) *Yuri's been in hospital since he had the accident.*

2 Leo bought his car three months ago.

   (*have*) ....

   ....

3 My uncle started to work for Microsoft a long time ago.

   (*work*) ....

   ....

4 The last time I saw Harry was a year ago.

   (*not see*) ....

   ....

5 Gary first met Eva in 2001.

   (*know*) ....

   ....

6 My cousin went to live in Bristol in 2002.

   (*live*) ....

   ....

4 Key expressions *Time expressions*

Complete the sentences. Use *for, since, during* or *ago*.

1 My grandfather fell asleep .... the film.

2 I haven't eaten .... breakfast.

3 This old clock was made a long time ....

4 I'll phone you .... the week.

5 I haven't been to the cinema .... ages.

6 I heard a lot of noises .... the night.

7 I haven't worn this shirt .... I bought it.

8 That song has been number one .... a fortnight.

5 Reading *Ellis Island*

Read the text about American immigrants. Then read the sentences and write *T* (true) or *F* (false).

Ellis Island is a small island in the bay of New York. A hundred years ago it was the place where new immigrants to the USA first arrived. Every year hundreds of ships full of immigrants came across the Atlantic from Europe. There were so many that the US government decided to build a special reception centre on Ellis Island.

On January 1st 1892 an Irish girl called Annie Moore was the first immigrant to pass through the centre. To mark the event, the immigration officers gave her a $10 gold coin. It was Annie's 15th birthday on the same day. 16 million people followed Annie through the doors of the centre between 1892 and 1954, when it was closed.

At the end of the 18th century, there were only 4 million people in the USA. But by 1900, the population had grown to 75 million. Ellis Island became the door to a new life for many Europeans.

When they arrived, the immigrants had a medical examination and an intelligence test. The ones who failed the tests (only 2% of the total) had to go back to Europe. Some of them jumped into the sea and tried to swim from the island to New York. The successful ones entered the USA and, after many difficulties, most of them stayed. Today, nearly half of all Americans are connected to someone who passed through Ellis Island.

1 Today, new immigrants enter the USA at the centre on Ellis Island.   ....

2 The reception centre at Ellis Island was built because of the great number of immigrants.   ....

3 Immigration officers gave Annie Moore a $10 gold coin as a birthday present.   ....

4 At the end of the 19th century, America's population was 75 million.   ....

5 To enter the USA, the immigrants had to pass a medical examination and an intelligence test.   ....

6 Most of the immigrants failed the tests.   ....

7 The ones who failed tried to swim from Europe to New York.   ....

8 Nearly 50% of Americans have a family connection with someone who arrived at Ellis Island.   ....

6 Extension *Time words*

Can you complete these words? They all refer to a period of time.

1 s _e_ _c_ _o_ _n_ d

2 m _ n _ _ e

3 _ _ u r

4 _ _ g h _

5 d _ _

6 w _ _ _

7 f _ _ t _ _ _ _ t

8 m _ _ t _

9 _ _ a r

10 c _ _ t _ _ y

1 Key vocabulary *Personal possessions*

Which is the odd one out? <u>Underline</u> one of the things in each group.

1 curry   carrot   comb   crisps

2 wedding   photo album   birthday party   holiday

3 purse   bag   rucksack   money

4 shampoo   brush   headache   hairdryer

5 stereo   MP3 player   camera   DVD player

6 bank card   coin   wallet   €20

7 clock   ring   watch   necklace

8 shoes   earrings   socks   boots

9 hat   coat   key ring   jacket

2 Superlatives 32

Complete the sentences. Use the superlative form of the adjectives in the box.

| noisy | weird | wet | interesting | ~~dry~~ | good |

1 The Atacama Desert is *the driest* place in the world.

2 Saturday will be .... day.

3 Sam is .... runner in the school.

4 I've just had .... dream! It was really strange.

5 They're .... family in the street.

6 My grandfather is .... person in our family.

3 Superlatives + present perfect + ever 6

Write B's question each time.

1 A: Jack's a good mountain climber.
   B: What / high mountain / climb?

   What's the highest mountain he's ever climbed?

2 A: We've seen some very strange animals.
   B: What / strange animal / see?

3 A: I love travelling.
   B: What / good place / visit?

4 A: I've made a lot of mistakes.
   B: What / bad mistake / make?

5 A: My two brothers love dangerous sports.
   B: What / dangerous thing / do?

6 A: She sometimes does really silly things.
   B: What / crazy thing / do?

4 give + direct and indirect object 24

Match 1–6 with a–f.

1 I gave Anna the photos.
2 I gave Jamie the wallet.
3 I gave you the keys.
4 I gave Susan the number.
5 I gave Danny and Nadia the money.
6 I gave John the stamps.

a I gave it to him.
b I gave it to her.
c I gave them to her.
d I gave them to him.
e I gave them to you.
f I gave it to them.

1 _c_   2 _____   3 _____   4 _____   5 _____   6 _____

5 Listening

Listen to Michelle giving three descriptions. What's she talking about? Write the correct letter (a–e).

a The most frightening thing she's ever done.
b The most interesting place she's ever visited.
c The worst holiday she's ever had.
d The strangest thing she's ever seen.
e The easiest decision she's ever made.

1 _____   2 _____   3 _____

6 Extension *Time to talk*

a Colin is having a conversation with a friend. Read what he says.

COLIN:
• I really like that jacket. How long have you had it?
• Where did you buy it?
• Do you usually buy your clothes there?
• Have you ever been to the market in Queen Street?
• I got this T-shirt at the market. It was only £3. What do you think of it?

Now listen to the conversation.

b Read Colin's sentences again. Then imagine he's talking to you. Think about the answers you want to make.

c Close your book, listen to the sentences and respond.

'On the move': Vocabulary check

1 Look at the words in the box. Can you find two adjectives that express negative feelings?

away from	confused	foreigner
feel at home	adapt	lonely
in some ways	in my blood	move

....

2 Complete the sentences. Use the words in the box in Exercise 1.

1 I've always loved the sea. I started sailing when I was very young. The sea's ....

2 Tamara's going to travel round Asia. She'll be .... home for three months.

3 Frank doesn't know anyone at his new evening class. He feels quite ....

4 I'm a bit .... Is Charles your cousin or your uncle?

5 Mrs Cook doesn't like living in the city. She wants to .... to the country.

6 Jessica went to live in the USA last year, but she doesn't .... there, so she's coming back to England soon.

7 .... I like Ellie, but we don't always get on well with each other.

8 My uncle's got a new job in Alaska, but he isn't enjoying it. He can't .... to the cold climate.

9 At first, Marek was a .... in a strange country, but now England is his home.

3 Translate these sentences into your language.

1 Boris broke his leg during the holidays, and he hasn't been to school for a fortnight.

....

....

....

2 A: How long have you known Adriana?
B: Since we were at primary school.

....

....

....

3 My cousin went to Australia a long time ago. I haven't seen him for ages.

....

....

....

4 I swam with dolphins in California. It's the best thing I've ever done.

....

....

....

5 A: I like this old guitar.
B: Yes, a friend gave it to me years ago, but I don't play it any more.

....

....

....

6 I gave Leo a birthday present, but he still hasn't said thank you.

....

....

....

Unit 6 Learning diary

Date _____

Now I know how to:

	Easy	Not bad	Difficult

- say how long something has continued, using *for* and *since* ☐ ☐ ☐

  Our football team hasn't won a match _____ last year.

  I've known my best friend _____ eight years.

  I've _____ for _____ .

- use time expressions. ☐ ☐ ☐

  I haven't been camping _____ ages.

  I fell asleep _____ my maths lesson.

  Have I missed the train?   Yes, it left three minutes _____ .

  Gary has been in hospital _____ a fortnight.

- talk about important events using superlative adjectives + *ever*. ☐ ☐ ☐

  What's the craziest thing you've _____ done?

  It's _____ I _____ seen.

- use a direct and an indirect object after *give*. ☐ ☐ ☐

  What did you give Adriana and Luis for their birthday? I gave Adriana _____

  _____ , and I gave _____ .

  Those are my schoolbooks. Can you give _____ to _____ ?

- write a personal account of my experiences. ☐ ☐ ☐

KEY WORDS
Personal possessions

brush _____   _____

_____   _____

_____   _____

_____   _____

_____

WORD WORK
still and *any more*

Sam hasn't got up yet. He's _____ in bed.

You can have this jacket. I don't wear it _____ .

7 Celebrations

1 Key vocabulary *Special occasions*

a Complete the greetings on the cards.

b Complete the sentences with words for special occasions.

1 I got lots of cards and p............................... on my birthday.

2 We went outside to watch the f............................... at midnight on New Year's Eve.

3 Beth and Andy have invited 90 g............................... to their wedding.

4 Mrs Gray is in the kitchen. She's making a c............................... for Danny's birthday.

5 At Christmas time, you see lots of d............................... in the shops, in the streets and in people's houses.

6 People wear fantastic c............................... at the carnival in Rio de Janeiro.

7 On 1st May there's a p............................... through the streets of our town.

8 It's my sister's tenth birthday, so there will be ten c............................... on the cake.

2 Reading *New Year in Scotland*

a Read the tourist information about Scotland. Then match the names of the three places with the photos (A–C).

Edinburgh .... Burghead .... Lewis ....

If you want a special start to the new year, you won't find a better place than Scotland.

- The country's biggest celebration takes place in **Edinburgh**. 100,000 people come to the city centre for a huge street party on New Year's Eve. This year there will be six bands playing different kinds of music. And at midnight you'll see some wonderful fireworks at Edinburgh Castle.

If you visit other places in Scotland, you'll discover some more unusual celebrations.

- In the village of **Burghead**, New Year is celebrated on 11th January! They have a very old tradition called the Burning of the Clavie. The Clavie is a heavy wooden barrel which is filled with small branches. Local men set the barrel on fire and carry it around the village to a castle on top of the hill. They say that if you can get a piece of burnt wood from the Clavie, you'll have good luck during the year.
- In the town of **Lewis**, they remember when Scotland was attacked by Vikings from Norway. They turn off the street lights and about 1,000 people walk together through the town in Viking clothes and helmets. They carry burning torches and they pull a Viking ship through the streets. Finally the ship is burnt in a huge fire, and after that there are parties all round the town.

You'll find more Scottish New Year celebrations if you look on our website.

b Read the text again. Then read the sentences and write *E* (Edinburgh), *B* (Burghead) or *L* (Lewis).

1 People wear special costumes. ....

2 They don't celebrate New Year at the normal time. ....

3 They make a big fire at the end of the procession. ....

4 You can hear lots of music. ....

5 There's a superstition connected with the celebration. ....

6 It's the largest New Year celebration in Scotland. ....

3 First conditional with *if* and *unless* 13

Match 1–6 with a–f and make sentences.

1 Clare won't be very happy
2 Danny will meet us at the café
3 If you don't feel better tomorrow,
4 Unless we leave soon,
5 Nadia will go to the barbecue
6 If everyone comes on Saturday,

a unless he has to work.
b we'll have 30 guests.
c we'll miss the train.
d if she can.
e I'll ring the doctor.
f if it rains on her birthday.

1 ....   2 ....   3 ....   4 ....   5 ....   6 ....

4 First conditional with *if* and *unless* 13

Write complete sentences using the correct verb forms.

1 If / I / go / into town / I / buy / some decorations

If I go into town, I'll buy some decorations.

2 Mum / help / me to make my costume / if / she / get / home early

3 If / you / not be / careful / you / drop / those glasses

4 I / not be able to / buy anything / if / the supermarket / not be / open

5 Unless / your friend / get here / soon / he / miss / the procession

6 We / have to / buy a cake / unless / Julie / decide / to make one

5 Extension   *If …*

In your notebook, complete these sentences.

1 I'll be happy if …
2 … unless it rains.
3 If … , I'll be very annoyed.
4 Tomorrow will be a good day for me unless …

1 will G→ 11a

Complete the sentences. Use *will, 'll* or *won't* with the verbs in the box.

see	be able	come	make	put on	be	pass

1 Don't worry. The bus .... soon.

2 Annie .... her exam. She hasn't done enough work.

3 Sit down and relax. I .... you a cup of tea.

4 When .... I .... you again?

5 Janet's phone isn't working so she ....
   .... to ring us.

6 A: You'll be hot in that sweater.

   B: Yes, you're right. I .... a T-shirt.

7 There .... many people at the beach. It's quite cold this morning.

2 going to G→ 11b

Complete the questions. Then write the answers.

1 A: What / she / do?

   What's she going to do?

   B: *She's going to wash the floor.*

2 A: What instrument / he / play?

   ....
   ....

   B: ....

3 A: What / they / do with the present?

   ....
   ....

   B: ....

4 A: What / you / have?

   ....

   B: ....

5 A: How / they / get home?

   ....
   ....

   B: ....

6 A: Who / he / ring?

   ....

   B: ....

3 will and going to G→ 11a, b

Circle the right answer: a or b.

1 What are your plans for this evening?
   a I'll write my geography essay.
   b I'm going to write my geography essay.

2 We need some candles for Sam's birthday cake.
   a OK. I'll buy some from the supermarket on my way home.
   b OK. I'm going to buy some from the supermarket on my way home.

3 I think we should get the train.
   a I agree. It'll be quicker than the bus.
   b I agree. It's going to be quicker than the bus.

4 Katherine says she's going to try mountain climbing.
   a Yes, but she probably won't enjoy it.
   b Yes, but she probably isn't going to enjoy it.

5 Why are you wearing shorts?
   a Because I'll go for a run.
   b Because I'm going to go for a run.

4 Listening A weather report

a 🔊 Listen to the weather report. On the map draw two weather symbols for Brighton and London. Use these symbols.

b 🔊 Listen again and write the temperatures for Brighton and London.

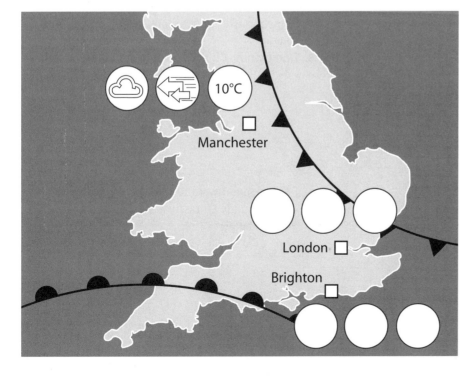

5 Key expressions I hope/guess so.

Complete the conversations with the expressions in the box.

| I hope so.   I hope not.   I guess so.   I guess not. |

1 A: You won't be able to take your surfboard. There won't be room for it in the car.

   B: No, ...

2 A: You'll look good in that dress.

   B: .... It cost a lot of money.

3 A: Will we have to take an umbrella?

   B: .... They say it will probably rain this evening.

4 A: It won't take long to get home from here.

   B: .... I'm really tired.

6 Extension The week ahead

Think about next week. Can you think of one example for each thing in this list?

1 a programme you're going to watch

   I'm going to watch ....

   ....

2 a piece of work you're going to finish

   ....

   ....

3 a person you'll probably see

   ....

   ....

4 something you'll do if you can

   ....

   ....

5 something you probably won't enjoy

   ....

   ....

'Invitations': Vocabulary check

1 Look at the words in the box. Can you find one verb of movement?

| fancy dress | just | afterwards | note | come over |
| outdoors | let me know | look after | look forward to |

....

2 Match the sentences.

1 I'll have an ice cream, please.
2 I always look forward to August.
3 I think I left my glasses at your house.
4 We're going on holiday for two weeks.
5 We can't have breakfast outdoors.
6 Why don't you come over to my house?
7 We won't have time to eat before the match.
8 I don't know where she's gone.
9 I don't think I'll go to the party.

a Let me know if you find them.
b But just a small one.
c I don't like wearing fancy dress.
d Look! It's raining.
e She didn't leave a note.
f Our neighbours are going to look after our cat.
g I'll show you my holiday photos.
h That's when I have my summer holiday.
i We'll have to have a meal afterwards.

1 .... 2 .... 3 .... 4 .... 5 .... 6 .... 7 .... 8 .... 9 ....

3 Translate these sentences into your language.

1 Be careful! If you break that mirror, you'll have bad luck.

....
....
....
....

4 A: Can you meet Gran this afternoon?
  B: Yes, I'll pick her up at the station.

....
....
....

2 A: If I come with you, will there be enough room in the car?
  B: I hope so.

....
....
....
....

5 A: Someone will have to look after the children tonight.
  B: Don't worry, I'll do that. It won't be a problem.

....
....
....

3 A: We won't want to eat outdoors unless the weather's nice.
  B: No, I guess not.

....
....
....

6 A: I'm looking forward to the party on New Year's Eve.
  B: Yes, it sounds fantastic. I'd love to come, but I'm afraid I can't.

....
....
....

Unit 7 Learning diary

Date _____

Now I know how to:

	Easy	Not bad	Difficult

- use *if* and *unless* to talk about future consequences. ☐ ☐ ☐

  _____ you don't hurry, we'll be late.

  We won't be able to go for a walk _____ it stops raining.

  What _____ we do if we _____ the last train?

- talk about the future using *will* and *going to*. ☐ ☐ ☐

  I _____ be 17 next Friday.

  I think Jane _____ like this record.

  Do you want to come to the shops with me? I _____ buy a new jacket.

- make offers. ☐ ☐ ☐

  Give me that box. I _____ carry it for you.

  I can't make dinner now. I'm too tired.   Don't worry. I _____ .

- react to what people say using *I hope/I guess* + *so/not*. ☐ ☐ ☐

  Do you think the exam will be easy?   I hope _____ .

  Martin's ill, He won't be able to play.   No, I guess _____ .

- write an invitation and a reply. ☐ ☐ ☐

KEY WORDS
Words for special occasions

cake _____ _____

_____ _____

_____

_____

WORD WORK
Verbs with *look*

look	*at*	a photo
look	_____	something you've lost
look	_____	a word in a dictionary
look	_____	someone who's ill
look	_____	a museum
look	_____	your next holiday

Secrets and lies

1 *might* and *may* 15

Complete the conversations with the replies (a–f).

a It may be hard to see him.	b Yes, I might put this on.
c He might see you.	d We might become film stars.
e They might interview us on television.	f He may come out in a minute.

A: If he comes out, I'll follow him.

B: ¹........ You'll need to use a disguise.

A: ²........

A: Look! He's turned the light off.

B: We must watch the door. ³........

A: Yes. It's very dark. ⁴........

A: It'll be good when we catch him.

B: Yes. ⁵........

A: And after that, who knows? ⁶........

2 *might/may* and *might not/may not* 15

Read the sentences and answer the questions. Use *might/ may* or *might not/may not* with the words in the box.

win	enjoy it	believe him	fly	rain	~~come~~

1 Emily's waiting for John outside the cinema. She's been there for 20 minutes. Why is she getting worried?

   Because he might not come.

2 Eva's going into town soon. Why is she taking an umbrella with her?

   ....

3 Richard's baseball team are playing in the Grand Final today. Why is he excited?

   ....

4 Maria's going to a party, but she isn't looking forward to it. Why?

   ....

5 Steve's made a model aeroplane, but he's a bit anxious about it. Why?

   ....

6 The police are interviewing Mark. He hasn't done anything wrong but he's still frightened. Why?

   ....

3 *when* in future sentences 12

Rewrite the sentences using *when* + present simple.

1 Karen will start her new job next month. She'll move to London.

   When Karen starts her new job, she'll
   move to London.

2 I'll get home soon. Then I'll ring Andrew.

   When I ....

   ....

3 Mrs Palmer will be 65 soon. Then she'll retire.

   When ....

   ....

4 I'll see Greg tomorrow. I'll give him your message.

   ....

   ....

5 Jack's going to work in the police department. He'll have to wear a uniform.

   ....

   ....

4 Dialogue completion

It's Saturday afternoon and Danny is working in Karim's shop. Complete the conversation. Circle the right answer: a, b or c.

KARIM: Danny, could you put these bottles in the fridge if [1]........ enough room?

DANNY: OK, no problem. It's not very busy today, is it?

KARIM: No. I [2]........ have time to clean the shelves this afternoon. But first I'll make us some tea.

DANNY: That's a good idea.

KARIM: What are you going to do when [3]........ work this evening?

DANNY: I don't know. [4]........ go out tonight. I'm feeling a bit tired.

KARIM: Well, you can leave early if we [5]........ many customers.

DANNY: Thanks, Karim. But [6]........ busy later [7]........ the football match finishes. If Liverpool win today, everyone will want to celebrate.

1 a they're
   b there's
   c there will be

2 a may
   b may not
   c won't

3 a you finish
   b you finished
   c you'll finish

4 a I'll
   b I might
   c I might not

5 a have
   b don't have
   c won't have

6 a we're
   b we might be
   c we may not be

7 a if
   b while
   c when

5 Listening *Jobs in the future*

a 🔊 Listen to four people talking about the kind of job they'd like to have in the future. Read the sentences and tick (✓) *Yes* or *No*.

		Yes	No
1	Eddie may go to university.	☐	☐
2	He might get some help from a relative.	☐	☐
3	Lucy isn't interested in teaching.	☐	☐
4	David wants to work with people who need help.	☐	☐
5	He thinks he'll earn a lot of money.	☐	☐
6	Fiona hopes she'll be able to go abroad.	☐	☐

b Decide which job would be the best for each person.

> pilot   nurse   TV reporter   shop assistant
> house painter   secretary   farmer   PE teacher
> private detective

Eddie: ....   Lucy: ....

David: ....   Fiona: ....

6 Extension *Time to talk*

a Nick is having a conversation with a friend. Read what he says.

NICK:
- How old will you be when you leave school?
- What will you do after that?
- Will you still live at home?
- I think I might live abroad when I'm older. What about you?
- Do you think you'll get married and have children?

🔊 Now listen to the conversation.

b Read Nick's sentences again. Then imagine he's talking to you. Think about the answers you want to make.

c 🔊 Close your book, listen to the sentences and respond.

1 Key vocabulary

Verbs and nouns that go together

<u>Underline</u> the right words.

1 Don't (*make / keep*) a promise to do something unless you're sure you can do it.

2 I don't believe their story. They often tell (*lies / the truth*).

3 If you break the (*law / promise*), you'll be in trouble with the police.

4 She promised to help us, but she didn't do anything. She didn't (*make / keep*) her promise.

5 If you tell Keith about this, he'll tell everyone in the class. He can't (*hold / keep*) a secret.

6 That's a lie! Why don't you (*say / tell*) the truth?

7 Liz will be here soon. She promised to come, and I'm sure she won't (*make / break*) her promise.

8 Don't worry if you (*make / do*) a mistake. You can correct it later.

2 Second conditional 14

Match 1–6 with a–f and write the correct verb form.

1 I'd ring Justine
2 If Olga kept her promises,
3 We'd go skiing
4 If you didn't go to bed late,
5 I wouldn't see Tim and Joe so often
6 If Jenny liked jazz,

a if there (*be*) enough snow.
b if they (*not live*) next door.
c you (*not feel*) tired all the time.
d if I (*have*) her number.
e she (*come*) to the concert.
f people (*trust*) her.

1 *d   had*

2 ....

3 ....

4 ....

5 ....

6 ....

3 Key expressions *Responding to opinions*

Complete the dialogue with the words in the box.

I don't agree.   Yes, exactly!
I know what you mean,   That's true, but

A: Mum, I think I'll take this sweater to the charity shop.

B: You can't do that! Your grandma made it for you.

A: ¹.. I can't wear it. It's for someone who's about eight years old.

B: ².. but you can't take it to the charity shop.

A: Why not? Gran won't know.

B: ³.. She might see it in the window. How would you feel if you were her?

A: I'd feel upset, I suppose.

B: ⁴..

4 *should/shouldn't* 19

Read these sentences that teenagers wrote about adults. Complete them with *should* or *shouldn't*.

1 Adults .... find time to talk to us.

2 They .... think that we're exactly like them.

3 They .... talk about us in front of other people.

4 They .... say sorry if they make a mistake.

5 They .... break their promises.

6 They .... respect our opinions.

5 Reading *Living in a shop window*

Read the text. Then read the sentences and circle the right answer: a, b or c.

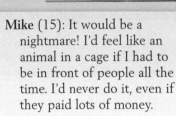

HARRODS, the famous London department store, is going to pay four people to live in their shop window for six days. They will use new electrical equipment that the shop is selling. Everyone in the street will be able to see them. Also, cameras will film them 24 hours a day so that people can watch them on Harrods' website.

We asked the Masons, a family from south London, if they would like to do this.

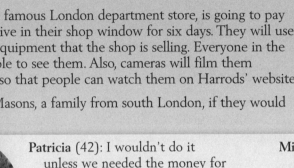

Patricia (42): I wouldn't do it unless we needed the money for something really important. I'll probably go and look at the window when the four people are there, but I wouldn't want to be one of them.

Mike (15): It would be a nightmare! I'd feel like an animal in a cage if I had to be in front of people all the time. I'd never do it, even if they paid lots of money.

Alice (16): I'd feel stupid in a shop window, and it would be embarrassing if my friends came to see me. But if Harrods gave me enough money, I guess I might do it. They'd have to offer at least £200,000! Then I might be interested.

Joe (8): If they asked me, I'd say yes. It would be fun and I'd be famous, like someone on TV. And the money would be great. I could get a mountain bike, and I'd buy some things for my family too.

1 At Harrods, four people ...
   a are going to live in the window.
   b will get some money to buy new equipment.
   c will be on TV every day.

2 Patricia ...
   a isn't interested in the Harrods window at all.
   b might live in the window for a special reason.
   c needed some money for something important.

3 Alice ...
   a will probably get thousands of pounds from Harrods.
   b would definitely live in the window if they offered her lots of money.
   c wouldn't do it unless she got lots of money.

4 Mike ...
   a often has to appear in front of people.
   b hasn't got a definite opinion.
   c certainly wouldn't live in the window.

5 Joe ...
   a would enjoy living in the window.
   b likes being on television.
   c is going to buy some presents for his family.

6 Extension

How should teenagers behave? Look again at Exercise 4 and write at least three sentences using *should* and *shouldn't*.

Teenagers should get lots of exercise. They shouldn't ...

'For sale?': Vocabulary check

1 Look at the words in the box. Can you find three words that are connected with money?

admire	cheque	fountain	deposit	liar	delighted	unfortunately	receipt	career	harbour

....

2 Match these definitions with the words in the box in Exercise 1.

1 When you think someone is wonderful, this verb describes your feelings for that person.

2 When you've paid for something, the shop assistant will give you this.

3 When you buy something, you can sometimes pay this if you don't have to pay the total price immediately.

4 You can use one of these to pay for something.

5 This is what you are if you don't tell the truth.

6 This sends water into the air.

7 Boats come here at the end of a journey.

8 The job or jobs you do during your working life.

9 This word means 'very pleased'.

10 This word is the opposite of 'luckily'.

3 Translate these sentences into your language.

1 A: What will you do when you leave school?
   B: I might look for a job in the police department.

2 Stephen has gone to Italy. He'll probably stay with Marco when he's in Rome.

3 A: Can you give this book back to Tamara?
   B: OK. But I'm not going out tonight, so I may not see her until the weekend.

4 You shouldn't tell lies and you should keep your promises.

5 A: Mrs Roberts really loves her job. She'd be bored if she retired.
   B: Yes, exactly.

6 A: What would you do if you found a purse in the street?
   B: I'd probably take it to the police station.

Unit 8 Learning diary

Date _____

Now I know how to:

	Easy	Not bad	Difficult

- talk about things that aren't certain, using *might* or *may*. ☐ ☐ ☐

  I'm not sure I'll go out tonight. I _____ stay at home.

  I _____ see you tomorrow because I have to go out with my parents.

  Next weekend I may _____ .

  I might not _____ .

- use *when* in future sentences. ☐ ☐ ☐

  He's going to leave school when he _____ 18.

  What places will you visit when you _____ to London?

- talk about hypothetical situations. ☐ ☐ ☐

  If you told me lies, I _____ be very pleased.

  Where would you go in the world if someone _____ you a free ticket?

  I _____ go _____ .

- respond to other people's opinions. ☐ ☐ ☐

  I don't think we should listen to other people's advice.   I _____ agree. They might be right.

  We can't be honest all the time.   That's _____ , but I think we should try.

- write a 'sales talk'. ☐ ☐ ☐

KEY WORDS

Verbs and nouns that go together

make	keep
a promise	_____
_____	_____
break	tell
_____	_____

WORD WORK

so and *because*

We didn't win _____ we played badly.

We played well, _____ we won easily.

9 Groups

1 Key vocabulary *People in groups*

Complete the crossword with words for groups of people.

Across

1 We've got a lot of good singers in our ....
4 On the night of the concert, there were 10,000 people in the ....
6 Winston plays the trumpet in a ....
7 There are nine players in a baseball ....

Down

1 There was a huge .... of people in the street.
2 About 30 musicians play in this ....
3 The Tigers are a local .... They sometimes have fights with other groups in the neighbourhood.
5 If you like acting, why don't you join the Drama .... ?

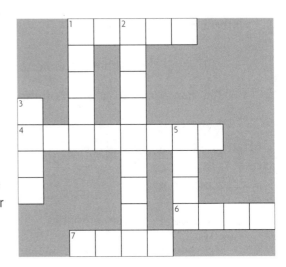

2 Verbs for likes and dislikes ⓖ 25a

Complete the sentences with the verbs in the box.

hate	mind
enjoy	prefer
stand	

1 I .... playing cards.

2 I .... getting up in the morning.

3 Skiing is fun, but I .... skating.

4 I can't .... going to the dentist.

5 I don't .... doing the housework.

3 Verb + *-ing* ⓖ 25b

Complete Suzanne's email. Use the prepositions in the box and the *-ing* form of the verbs.

| in | to | on | ~~for~~ | about | at |

To: robert.banks@fastmail.com
From: sfuller@gomail.co.uk

Hi Robert!

Thanks ¹ *for inviting* (invite) me to your place on Saturday. I'd love to come and I'm looking forward ² .... (see) you. You don't have to worry ³ .... (drive) me home. Mum's going to pick me up at 11.30.

I'll bring some information about the Sports Club. I'm definitely going to join. I'm useless ⁴ .... (run) but I'm quite keen ⁵ .... (do) gymnastics and I'm interested ⁶ .... (try) karate too. How about joining the club with me?

Love,
Suzanne

4 like / would ('d) like / want (G) → 25a

Read the sentences and underline the right words.

1 Luke (*enjoys* / *wants*) being in the school orchestra.
2 He doesn't (*want* / *like*) to join the football team.
3 (*He loves* / *He'd love*) to become a professional photographer.

4 (*Do* / *Would*) you like to take part in the maths competition?
5 Clare doesn't (*like* / *want*) studying at night.
6 (*I* / *I'd*) hate to be a pilot. I get nervous in planes.

5 Reading *Numerology*

Read the text about numerology. Then read the sentences (a–e) and match the people with the numbers (1–9).

Can your name tell you about your personality?
People who believe in numerology say YES!

Match the letters in your name with the numbers in the table. Add the numbers together until you get a total. Add again until you get a number from 1 to 9. Then check the description of your number.

Example: TOM HILL
$$2 + 6 + 4 + 8 + 9 + 3 + 3 = 35$$
$$3 + 5 = \boxed{8}$$

1 – A, J, S	6 – F, O, X
2 – B, K, T	7 – G, P, Y
3 – C, L, U	8 – H, Q, Z
4 – D, M, V	9 – I, R
5 – E, N, W	

1 You're independent and confident. You like being a leader and you're good at solving problems.

2 You're a sensitive person and you work well with other people. You don't like having arguments or making big decisions.

3 You're very good at communicating. You're an optimistic, sociable person who loves life.

4 You're loyal, honest and hard-working. You think carefully and you're a good organiser.

5 You've got a lot of different skills and you're a quick thinker. You love feeling free and you enjoy travelling.

6 You're close to your family and interested in relationships. You're friendly, generous and helpful.

7 You're a serious person. You're good at studying difficult subjects and you're interested in discovering the truth.

8 You've got lots of energy and you're good at planning and organising. You'll probably be successful in business.

9 You've got strong feelings and you want to help the world. You're also very artistic, with a great imagination.

a Matt feels comfortable when he's in a team. He hates arguing with people. ☐

b Joanna paints wonderful pictures and she also writes music. ☐

c Adrian really enjoys talking to people and he loves going to parties. ☐

d Jenny does scientific research. For most people, her work is hard to understand, but she loves it. ☐

e Tony often goes abroad. He can't stand routines and he doesn't like staying in one place. ☐

6 Extension *Your number*

Look again at the text in Exercise 5. What's the number for your name? Do you think the description is right? Write at least two sentences in your notebook.

Yes, I like working with other people. For example, I love team sports. But I don't mind having an argument when I disagree with someone.

1 want someone to do something (G)→ 23

Match the sentences.

1 I can't go out this evening.
2 Could you come over here?
3 Charlotte doesn't want to ring Leo.
4 I think I'll phone my parents.
5 They aren't going to invite Sarah.
6 We're going for a walk.

a She wants him to ring her.
b They don't want her to come.
c My aunt wants me to babysit.
d Mum wants us to get some exercise.
e I want you to help me.
f I don't want them to worry about me.

1 ....   2 ....   3 ....   4 ....   5 ....   6 ....

2 want / don't want someone to do something (G)→ 23

Complete the sentences using the words in brackets.

1 The woman wants *Chris to help her* _____ (*help her*). She wants *him to carry her bag upstairs* _____ (*carry her bag upstairs*).

2 He wants _____ _____ (*go home*). He doesn't want _____ (*follow him*).

3 Sam's parents want _____ _____ (*work hard*). They want _____ (*be a doctor*).

4 My mum _____ _____ (*go out tonight*). She _____ (*babysit*).

3 ask / tell someone to do something (G) → 23

Rewrite the sentences with *asked* or *told*.

1 MY DAD: 'Turn the television off.'

(tell) *Dad told me to turn the television off.*

2 TEACHER: 'Finish the exercise for homework.'

(tell) *Our teacher* _____ *us*

_____ .

3 PAUL: 'Lisa, could you get some decorations for the party?'

(ask) *Paul* _____

_____ .

4 MR MARSHALL: 'Nadia, would you close the door?'

(ask) _____

_____

5 MRS GRAY: 'You must be home early, Danny.'

(tell) _____

_____

6 MY FRIEND LIZ: 'Could you ring Debbie, please?'

(ask) _____

_____

4 Key expressions

Requests and responses

Underline the right words in the requests. Then choose the best replies from the list (a–h).

1 NADIA: Clare, can (*I lend / you lend me*) your calculator for a minute?

CLARE: .... Here you are.

2 MAN: Excuse me. (*Could you / Would you mind*) tell me the time, please?

DANNY: ....

3 MR GRAY: Andy, we've got a problem with our computer. (*I want you to / Would you*) come and have a look at it?

ANDY: .... Beth and I are going out this evening. I can come tomorrow if you like.

4 WOMAN: (*Would you / Would you mind*) closing the window?

LUKE: ....

a I guess not.
b Yes, it's twenty past nine.
c Yes, sure.
d Yes, I do.
e No way!
f No, of course not.
g I guess so.
h I'm afraid I can't.

5 Listening

🔊 Listen to the conversations. Tick (✓) the right answer: A, B or C.

1 Which sports group might Angela join?

A ☐   B ☐   C ☐

2 On Sunday, which group will Louise be in?

A ☐   B ☐   C ☐

3 What does Jack's father want him to do?

  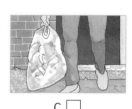

A ☐   B ☐   C ☐

6 Extension *Requests*

In your notebook, write a request to each of these people, asking him/her to do something for you.

1 *Can you lend me your camera?*

1 a friend   2 a neighbour   3 a teacher   4 a member of your family

'Living together': Vocabulary check

1 Look at the words in the box. Can you find a preposition?

ant   beside   brave   defend   fox   jaws   nest   sharp   ....

2 Match the pictures with the words in the box in Exercise 1.

1 .... 2 .... 3 .... 4 ....

5 .... 6 .... 7 .... 8 ....

3 Translate these sentences into your language.

1 Monica loves being in the choir, but she isn't keen on singing in front of a big audience.

2 I'd like to take part in the play, but I'm useless at acting. I'm not confident enough.

3 A: What do you want me to do?
B: Would you lend me €10?

4 Could you come over here? I want you to take a photo of me and Sophie.

5 A: Mum wants you to take the dog for a walk.
B: Can you tell Emma to take him? I'm too tired.

6 A: Excuse me, would you mind sitting over there?
B: No, of course not. No problem.

Unit 9 Learning diary

Date _____

Now I know how to:

	Easy	Not bad	Difficult

- use *-ing* after certain verbs and after prepositions. ☐ ☐ ☐

    I'm a sociable person. I don't like _____ on my own.

    I enjoy cooking, but I can't stand _____ the washing up.

    I'd love to be in a band, but I'm useless at _____ the guitar.

    I hate travelling by car because I worry about _____ sick.

- use the right word order after *want*, *ask* and *tell*. ☐ ☐ ☐

    What do you want me to do?   I want _____ take the dog for a walk.

    I won't see you at the weekend because Harry has asked _____ go camping with him.

    Martha was really angry when I told _____ stop being selfish.

    My parents want _____.

- make and respond to polite requests. ☐ ☐ ☐

    Could you _____ the way to the supermarket?   Yes, of _____.

    I can't open this bottle. Would you mind _____ it for me?   No, _____ not.

    Would you _____?

- write a TV commentary about teenagers. ☐ ☐ ☐

KEY WORDS

People in groups

gang _____   _____

_____   _____

_____   _____

_____

WORD WORK

too and *enough* with adjectives

I can't translate these sentences. They're _____ difficult.

You mustn't dive into the swimming pool. The water isn't deep _____.

10 Food for thought

1 Key vocabulary *Food*

Write the words.

1 These vegetables are long and green.

   b *eans*

2 They're orange vegetables and they grow under the ground.

   c.....................................

3 They're very small, round, green vegetables. We often buy them in packets from the freezer at the supermarket.

   p.....................................

4 This is a kind of meat from a bird.

   c.....................................

5 They aren't fish, but they live in the sea. They're pink when they're cooked.

   p.....................................

6 It's a large green vegetable. We eat the flower, not the leaves.

   b.....................................

7 This green vegetable is used for salad. We don't cook it.

   l.....................................

8 This is the main food of Asia. It's grown in fields with lots of water.

   r.....................................

9 It's made from milk. It's usually white or yellow and there are hundreds of different kinds.

   c.....................................

10 They're red fruit which are eaten in summer. They grow on the ground, not on trees.

   s.....................................

2 *some, any, a lot of*

Complete the sentences with *some, any* and *a lot of*.

I've bought [1] _a lot of_ food today, so I hope there's room for it in the fridge. There's [2].......................... bread in this bag, if you're hungry. I couldn't find [3].......................... strawberries today — in fact I didn't buy [4].......................... fruit. I got [5].......................... lovely tomatoes and [6].......................... cheese for lunch. There were [7].......................... people in town. I spent [8].......................... time standing in queues!

3 *any* and *no* G→ 34

Look at the pictures and answer the questions. Use *any* or *no* and the words in the box.

| snow | petrol | teeth | big hills | legs | oxygen |

1 Why is it easy to ride a bike in Holland?

   Because there are ....

   ....

2 Why don't people go skiing in the north of Australia?

   Because there isn't ....

   ....

3 Why can't snakes run?

   Because they've got ....

4 Why do astronauts need space-suits to survive on the moon?

   Because there's ....

   ....

5 Why are solar cars good for the environment?

   Because they don't use ....

   ....

6 Why can't birds bite?

   Because they've got ....

   ....

4 less, fewer, more 33

Write two sentences about each of these world facts. Use *more*, *less* or *fewer*.

1 China grows 31% of the world's rice. India grows 20%.

China grows <u>*more rice than India.*</u>

India grows <u>*less rice than China.*</u>

2 London has about 610 mm of rain a year. Sydney has about 1,100 mm.

London has ....

....

Sydney has ....

....

3 The Boeing 747 carries 450 passengers. The Boeing 777 carries 390.

The Boeing 747 carries ....

....

The Boeing 777 carries ....

....

4 Brazil produces 35% of the world's coffee. Colombia produces 12%.

Brazil produces ....

....

Colombia produces ....

....

5 In the UK, there are about 28 million men and 31 million women.

There are ....

....

There are ....

....

5 Listening

A farmers' market

🔊 Listen to part of a radio programme about a new market. Complete the advertisement with the right information.

Hartfield Farmers' Market

Fresh products from local farms not more than [1].......................... **miles away**

Products for sale include: meat, vegetables, flowers, [2].......................... , eggs, bread

Place: King's [3]..........................

Time: first [4].......................... of the month

9.00 am – [5].......................... pm

Contact: Rosemary Barton tel: 01523 [6]..........................

6 Extension *Codeword*

All the words in this puzzle are food words. Each letter has a number. You know the numbers for *O*, *A* and *C*, so fill in these letters first. Then look for the food words. Write them in the puzzle and write the letters in the table.

1	2	3	4	5	6	7	8	9	10	11	12	13	14	15	16	17
	O		A						C							

1 Funny questions

Match the questions with the answers and make eight jokes.

1 What goes up and down but never moves?
2 What starts with T, ends with T and has T inside?
3 What's got four legs but can't walk?
4 What kind of motorbike laughs?
5 Why do you keep your trumpet in the fridge?
6 What did one wall say to another wall?
7 Which are the biggest ants?
8 Which two letters contain nothing?

a Because I like cool music.
b A Yamaha ha! ha!
c Giants.
d 'I'll meet you at the corner.'
e Stairs.
f Two pairs of trousers.
g MT.
h A teapot.

1 .... 2 .... 3 .... 4 .... 5 .... 6 .... 7 .... 8 ....

2 Subject and object questions G⟶ 27

Put the words in the right order and make questions. How many of the questions can you answer? (The answers are all in the Student's Book.)

1 Danny / for / who / does / work ?

   Who does Danny work for?

   Karim.

2 married / who / to / got / Beth ?

3 do / does / Mary Martin / what ?

4 most / possession / Winston's / what's / precious ?

5 a photo / took / a school trip / on / who ?

6 to / who / class / her / gave / a talk ?

7 Andy / does / kind of / ride / what / motorbike ?

3 Subject and object questions G⟶ 27

Make questions to go with B's answers.

1 A: (What / lions?)

   What do lions eat?

   B: They eat meat.

2 A: (Who / the Mona Lisa?)

   B: Leonardo da Vinci painted it.

3 A: (What / kind of fruit / you?)

   B: I like strawberries, apples and grapes.

4 A: (Who / John Booth?)

   B: He killed Abraham Lincoln.

5 A: (Which / animals / grass?)

   B: Cows, horses and sheep eat it.

6 A: (Who / geography at your school?)

   B: Mr Carroll. He also teaches history.

4 Reading Better school meals

Jamie Oliver, a well-known cook, has made a TV show about lunches that are served to students in British schools. Read the text and then answer the questions.

Jamie's School Dinners was a television show that tried to change young people's ideas about food. The idea came from the chef Jamie Oliver. He wanted to make a series of programmes about the lunches that are served in school canteens.

Jamie was upset when he discovered that lots of schools were serving almost no fresh food. Their meals came out of packets – frozen burgers, pizzas, chips and sausages. Jamie wanted to show that it's possible to make good healthy meals that don't cost much. So he started cooking for a school in a poor area of south London.

There were lots of problems. The cooks in the canteen didn't believe his ideas would work. Jamie found that he needed more money to buy good food. And at first the students refused to eat the meals he cooked. They wanted the food they knew. Many of them never ate healthy meals at home. Some students couldn't identify an onion and didn't know what carrots or broccoli were.

Finally, however, they discovered that they preferred Jamie's meals. And teachers found that after eating his food, their students were able to think and work better.

The TV programmes were very popular. On his website, Jamie collected a list of nearly 280,000 people who supported his campaign. After that, the government promised to spend more money on better school meals. More action is needed, but things are certainly improving.

1 Who first thought of the idea for the TV programmes?

----

2 Name four types of food that school canteens were serving.

----

3 What did Jamie Oliver want to serve?

----

4 Who didn't think his plans would be successful?

----

5 Why didn't the students want to eat Jamie's food at first?

----

6 Did they like his cooking in the end?

----

7 How many people supported Jamie's campaign?

----

8 What was the result of this campaign?

----

5 Extension *Time to talk*

a Alison is having a conversation with a friend. Read what she says.

ALISON:

- Where does your family usually buy food? Do you go to the supermarket?
- What sort of food do you like?
- Do you eat much fruit?
- I quite enjoy cooking sometimes. Do you?
- So who usually does the cooking in your home?
- And who does the washing up?

🔊 Now listen to the conversation.

b Read Alison's questions again. Then imagine she's talking to you. Think about the answers <u>you</u> want to make.

c 🔊 Close your book, listen to the sentences and respond.

'Fast food nation': Vocabulary check

1 Look at the words in the box. Find a word with this stress pattern.

● ● ● ● _____

> best-selling   soft drink   taste (*n*)
> depressing   chemicals   smell   convenient
> fat   taste (*v*)   overweight

2 Complete the sentences. Use the words in the box in Exercise 1.

1 You use your nose to find out if you like the

_____ of something.

2 You put something in your mouth to find out if

you like the _____ .

3 _____ means 'too heavy'.

4 The word _____

describes a book that a lot of people buy.

5 Lemonade is a popular _____ .

6 The word _____ describes

something that gives you unhappy feelings.

7 _____ are often

added to our food and drink.

8 If you want a quick lunch, a fast food restaurant

is very _____ .

9 You shouldn't eat too much butter and cheese

because they contain a lot of _____ .

10 We enjoy eating things that _____

good.

3 Translate these sentences into your language.

1 I went to the market, but I couldn't find any olives and there were no fresh prawns.

_____

_____

_____

2 We made less money at the concert this year because we sold fewer tickets.

_____

_____

_____

3 A: Would you like a cold drink? There's some apple juice in the fridge.
   B: No, thanks. I'd prefer a cup of coffee.

_____

_____

_____

4 A: Who gave you those earrings?
   B: My sister. She gave them to me for my birthday.

_____

_____

_____

5 A: Who wants to watch the 10 o'clock news?
   B: Not me! The news is always so depressing.

_____

_____

_____

6 A: Did you enjoy the film?
   B: No, I was bored, and all my friends thought it was boring too.

_____

_____

_____

Unit 10 Learning diary

Date _____

Now I know how to:

	Easy	Not bad	Difficult

- use expressions of quantity. ☐ ☐ ☐

  There are no eggs in the fridge. = _____ any eggs in the fridge.

  We must go to the market. We've got _____ food in the house.

  He goes to work on his scooter. It uses _____ fuel than his car.

  The town's quieter in the winter. There are _____ tourists than in the summer.

  You're lucky. You've got _____ free time than me.

- express preferences. ☐ ☐ ☐

  I'd prefer to stay at home this evening. = I'd _____ stay at home this evening.

  What would you _____ to be, an actor or a musician?

  I don't mind going to the sports centre, but I'd rather _____ .

- make subject or object questions with *What, Who* and *Which*. ☐ ☐ ☐

  Ow! It fell on my head.   What _____ on your head?

  Who _____ these photos?   One of my sister's friends took them, I think.

  Which football team _____ you _____ ?   I support Chelsea.

  Who _____ they _____ to their party?   Everyone in the class.

- write a review of a place. ☐ ☐ ☐

KEY WORDS

Food

strawberries _____

_____

_____

_____

_____

_____

_____

_____

WORD WORK

Adjectives ending in *-ed/-ing*

A feeling

interested _____

excited _____

_____

_____

_____

_____

A description

interesting _____

_____

_____

_____

_____

_____

11 Challenges

1 Key vocabulary *Feelings*

Complete the sentences with adjectives.

1 I should go. Mum will be
a *nnoyed* _____ if I'm late for dinner.

2 Annie's going to sing in front of a big
audience tonight. She's feeling
n_____ .

3 My mobile started ringing during the
concert. I felt really e_____ !

4 Graham was very u_____ when
his cat died.

5 I'm f_____ u_____ . I've been in this
queue for almost an hour.

6 Jenny didn't know anyone at her new
school, so she was l_____ at
first.

7 I'm w_____ about Simon. He
doesn't look happy. I think something's
wrong.

8 Adam thought he might fail his exam. He
was very r_____ when he
discovered he'd passed.

9 I've bought a silver necklace for Natalie. I
hope she'll be p_____ .

10 We were hoping to see you last night. We
were d_____ when you
didn't come.

11 Dad looks very r_____ . He's
sitting in the sun and he's reading the
newspaper.

12 Kelly doesn't know we're coming. I bet
she'll be s_____ when we arrive.

2 Past perfect: affirmative Ⓖ➤ 10

Last night these people were thinking about events
that had happened during the day. Complete the
sentences. Use verbs from box A in the past perfect
and words from box B.

A	break have
	find get up
	walk ~~score~~

B	very early her favourite bowl
	~~a goal~~ home in the rain
	an argument a bone

1 Robbie was pleased because he *'d scored a goal.* _____

2 Maria was upset because she _____
_____ with her friend.

3 Mrs Davis was annoyed because she _____
_____ .

4 Mr Davis was wet because he _____
_____ .

5 Simon was tired because he _____
_____ that morning.

6 The dog was happy because it _____
_____ .

3 Past perfect: affirmative and negative Ⓖ➤ 10

Complete the text about a farm in Australia. Use the affirmative or negative form of the past perfect.

In September the rain finally arrived. Before that, we ¹............................... (have)

three years of dry weather. Day after day the sky ²............................... (be) blue

and almost no rain ³............................... (fall). We ⁴............................... (see)

any water in the river for over a year and the fields ⁵............................... (turn)

brown. So when the rain came, we were very relieved. We were lucky that the dry forests ⁶...............................

(catch) fire. Many of our sheep ⁷............................... (die), but the farm ⁸............................... (survive).

4 Reading 'Spiderman' at Canary Wharf

Read the text about Alain Robert. Then read the sentences and write T (true), F (false) or ? (the answer isn't in the text).

A French climber known as 'Spiderman' was rescued from a 50-floor office building in East London yesterday. He was halfway up the Canary Wharf Tower when he started to have difficulties.

Alain Robert, 40, is famous for climbing some of the world's tallest buildings. He had climbed to the 35th floor of the Canary Wharf Tower when he realised that he could not continue because of the wind and the rain. So he was brought to the ground in a lift which is used for cleaning windows. Police, fire fighters and an ambulance had already arrived at the scene.

It was Mr Robert's second visit to the tower at Canary Wharf. The first time, seven years ago, his climb had been successful and he had reached the top of the building.

He has climbed more than 30 skyscrapers around the world, including the Eiffel Tower in Paris, the Empire State Building in New York and the Petronas Towers in Kuala Lumpur, Malaysia. When he climbs, he uses no ropes or other equipment – he uses only his hands and feet.

Mr Robert's unusual career started at the age of 12. He discovered that he had forgotten the key to his flat on the eighth floor. He solved the problem by climbing up the building to get home.

1 The Canary Wharf Tower is a tall building in England. ....

2 When Alain climbed the building, there were lots of office workers inside. ....

3 He had problems because the weather was bad. ....

4 The police arrived when Alain got to the ground. ....

5 He's never climbed to the top of the Canary Wharf Tower. ....

6 He's climbed other buildings in London. ....

7 Yesterday he used special climbing equipment to make sure he was safe. ....

8 He climbed a building for the first time because he had forgotten his key. ....

5 Extension More feelings

Add vowels (a, e, i, o or u) and find eight adjectives for feelings.

| brd | nhppy | xctd | ntrstd | sd | ngry | shckd | rrttd |

1 .... 3 .... 5 .... 7 ....

2 .... 4 .... 6 .... 8 ....

1 must, can't, might, could (G) → 18

Read the conversation and <u>underline</u> the right words.

NADIA: Luke had his driving test this morning, didn't he?

DANNY: Yes, that's right. He promised to ring me if he passed, but he hasn't called.

NADIA: Oh. That ¹(*must / can't*) mean he failed. Poor Luke!

DANNY: Yes, he ²(*can't / must*) be really disappointed.

NADIA: I wonder where he is.

DANNY: I don't know. He ³(*could / can't*) be at home, but he isn't answering his phone.

NADIA: He ⁴(*could / can't*) be very happy on his own. I think we should try to find him.

DANNY: Yes. He ⁵(*must / might*) feel better if he's with us.

LUKE: Hi, guys!

NADIA: Oh, there you are, Luke! Hey, we're really sorry you failed the test.

LUKE: You ⁶(*can't / might*) be serious! I passed easily. I've just driven to Manchester in Dad's car. No problem!

2 must and can't for speculation (G) → 18

One word in each of these sentences is wrong! Correct them using *can't* and *must* and a word from the box.

| orchestra | scooters | ~~student~~ | waiter | flat |

1 Amy's a teacher at a university and she's taking her exams next month.

She _can't be a teacher. She must be a_ _student._

2 John's a pilot who serves meals at the Seaview Café.

He ....

....

3 Teresa lives in a house on the fourth floor.

It ....

....

4 Our school choir has got eight people who play the violin.

It ....

....

5 These motorbikes have a top speed of 50 kilometres an hour.

They ....

....

3 must, can't, might, could (G) → 18

Read Petra's description and look at the picture. Then complete the sentences. Use the words in the box.

| could | must (x 2) | can't (x 3) | might |
| father | mother | cousin | |

PETRA: My aunt Jenny took this photo on my brother Liam's 21st birthday. That's me with the hat. You can see Dad and Mum, and there's Liam and my sister Susie – she's the one with the sunglasses. The others are my cousin Jane and her boyfriend.

A can't be Petra because she isn't wearing a hat. She ¹........................ be Susie because she isn't wearing glasses.

So she ²........................ be Petra's ³........................ .

B ⁴........................ be Jenny, because Jenny took the photo. So she ⁵........................ be Petra's ⁶........................ .

C ⁷........................ be Liam or he ⁸........................ be Jane's boyfriend. He ⁹........................ be Petra's

¹⁰........................ because he's too young.

4 Key expressions *So/Neither ... I* G→ 28

Complete the dialogue. Use *So/Neither ... I.*

A: The cycling race is on TV today. They're going to ride more than 150 kilometres through the mountains.

B: I don't fancy doing that.

A: ¹ *Neither* _____ . But I'm looking forward to watching it on TV.

B: ² _____ .

A: There's a programme about scuba-diving later.

B: Oh, yes? I haven't tried scuba-diving but it must be interesting. I've got some good videos about life under the sea.

A: ³ _____ . But diving would be quite difficult, I think. I'm not a very good swimmer.

B: No, ⁴ _____ . I really think it's better to watch these things on TV.

A: Yes, ⁵ _____ .

5 Listening *Three conversations*

🔊 Listen to the three conversations. Circle the right answer: a, b or c.

Conversation 1

1 The man is
   a worried.
   b travelling by ferry.
   c on a sailing boat.

2 He thinks that
   a the boat can't be safe.
   b he could be seasick.
   c he might not get to Greece.

Conversation 2

3 Tom must be
   a good at climbing.
   b on top of a mountain.
   c afraid of heights.

4 When he got to the top, he was
   a pleased.
   b disappointed.
   c relieved.

Conversation 3

5 The girl says that tourist trips in space
   a will never happen.
   b might happen one day.
   c are only for millionaires.

6 She
   a has been in a spaceship.
   b thinks she'd enjoy being in a spaceship.
   c would like to see the Earth from space.

6 Extension *Who stole the money?*

Can you find the answer to this puzzle?

> Someone stole some money. The police knew that the person who took it was Alex, Bob or Carl. When the police asked questions, this is what the boys said:
>
> **ALEX:** I didn't do it.
> **BOB:** Carl did it.
> **CARL:** Bob's lying.
>
> Only <u>one</u> of the boys was telling the truth – the other two were lying.
>
> Who stole the money?

It can't be _____ or _____ .

It must be _____ .

'On the edge': Vocabulary check

1 Look at the words in the box. Can you find three words that express something unpleasant?

reach	disaster	rope	crawl	guilty	hop	weight	pain	manage

....

2 a Look at the pictures and complete the sentences. Use the verbs in the box in Exercise 1.

1 She had to .... to the car.

2 He didn't .... to finish the race.

3 She really wants to .... the top.

4 He had to .... across the ice.

b Match these sentences with the other words in the box in Exercise 1.

1 This hurts!   ....

2 You need this if you're a mountain climber.   ....

3 You may feel like this if you've done something bad.   ....

4 This word describes a terrible event.   ....

5 When we talk about this, we use grams and kilograms.   ....

3 Translate these sentences into your language.

1 When I got to the station, my friends had already left.

   ....

   ....

2 There was water all over the floor because someone hadn't closed the door of the fridge properly.

   ....

   ....

3 A: I want to sail round the world.
   B: So do I. It must be a fantastic experience.

   ....

   ....

   ....

4 A: Who's Maggie talking to?
   B: I don't know. It could be Terry or it might be Paul.

   ....

   ....

   ....

5 I was very embarrassed yesterday because my sister had read my diary.

   ....

   ....

   ....

6 A: I'm not going to try bungee-jumping.
   B: Neither am I. I'm sure it can't be safe.

   ....

   ....

   ....

Unit 11 Learning diary

Date _____

Now I know how to:

	Easy	Not bad	Difficult

- use the past perfect to talk about the past. ☐ ☐ ☐

  The house was very quiet. Everyone _____ gone to bed.

  I was tired yesterday morning because I _____ slept well the night before.

  Alex was really angry with Tom.   Why? What _____ Tom done?

- make speculations using *must, can't, might* and *could*. ☐ ☐ ☐

  The dog _____ like chocolate because it's eaten all the chocolate biscuits.

  You _____ be tired! You've just got out of bed.

  I haven't seen Dave today.   He might be ill, or he _____ be on holiday.

- show agreement and similarity, using *So* and *Neither*. ☐ ☐ ☐

  I'm really cold.   So _____ I.

  I love swimming.   So _____ I.

  My brother doesn't like going to the dentist.   _____ do I.

  I haven't got any brothers or sisters.   Neither _____ I.

- write a short story. ☐ ☐ ☐

KEY WORDS

Adjectives describing feelings

fed up _____   _____

_____   _____

_____   _____

_____   _____

WORD WORK

Adverbs

ADJECTIVE	ADVERB
slow	_____
successful	_____
safe	_____
quick	_____
angry	_____
good	_____
fast	_____
early	_____
hard	_____
late	_____

12 Happy endings

1 Key vocabulary *Money*

These sentences are wrong! Put the underlined words in the right sentences.

1 I'll have some money tomorrow, but today I'm <u>spend</u>! ......*broke*......

2 Natalie's got almost £1,000 in her <u>change</u>. ....

3 I'm not going to <u>borrow</u> all my money. I want to put some in the bank. ....

4 I need some money. Could I <u>broke</u> a few pounds until tomorrow? ....

5 We'll need some <u>cashpoint</u> if we want to get some chocolate from that machine. ....

6 You can get some money from the <u>credit card</u> at the supermarket. ....

7 I can <u>afford</u> you some money if you haven't got enough. ....

8 Dad used his <u>bank account</u> to pay for the petrol. ....

9 I'd love to buy that shirt, but it's £35! I can't <u>lend</u> it. ....

2 Reported speech G→ 21

Read the reported sentences. Then write what the people actually said.

He said it was a fabulous machine.

She said she wanted to buy a Harley.

She said she'd pay by credit card.

He said they were going to Memphis.

He said he couldn't find his wallet.

She said she didn't have any change.

3 Reported speech (G)→ 21

Read Justin's words. Then answer the
questions about what Justin said. Start each
sentence with *He said*.

> I won't be able to go on the camping trip, I'm
> afraid. I'm going to Holland. I want to visit
> some friends in Amsterdam, so I'm going to
> spend a few days there. They're great people.
> I'll probably go by coach – I can't afford to fly.

A: What did Justin say about the camping trip?

B: ¹ *He said he wouldn't be able to go.*

A: Why not? Did he tell you?

B: Yes. ² *He said* ....

....

A: I wonder why he's going there.

B: ³ ....

....

A: Is he going to stay there for a long time?

B: No. ⁴ ....

....

A: What did he say about his friends?

B: ⁵ ....

....

A: How's he going to get there? Do you know?

B: Yes. ⁶ ....

....

A: I think he should go by plane. It's much quicker.

B: ⁷ ....

....

4 Listening *At the station*

a 🔊 Listen to the conversation that Gary had
with Emma last Friday. Who's going to travel on
the train? ....

b 🔊 Listen again and tick (✓) the right answer:
true or false.

		true	false
1	Emma said the train was going to arrive at platform 5.	☐	☐
2	Gary was worried because no one was selling tickets.	☐	☐
3	Emma said that he could get his ticket from a machine.	☐	☐
4	She told him that the ticket cost £10.	☐	☐
5	Gary didn't have any change.	☐	☐
6	He lent Emma some money.	☐	☐

5 Extension *Poem*

🔊 Find the missing words and complete
the poem. Then listen to the poem and read
it aloud.

brk	bnk	cshpnt	~~spnt~~
lnd	crdt	brrwd	ffrd

I've ¹ ___*spent*___ my pocket money,

It disappeared like smoke.

I can't ² _____ a sandwich

As I'm now completely ³ _____ .

I tried to use the ⁴ _____ ,

But then my spirits sank:

My ⁵ _____ card is useless

And there's nothing in the ⁶ _____ .

I've borrowed from my brother,

I've ⁷ _____ from my mum.

I really need some money,

So could you ⁸ _____ me some?

Reported speech Ⓖ→ 21a

Complete the table with the right form of the verbs.

Direct speech	Reported speech
1 'I'm in the kitchen.'	She said she .... in the kitchen.
2 'I've got some fish for dinner.'	She said she .... some fish for dinner.
3 'I don't usually make the dinner.'	She said she .... usually .... the dinner.
4 'I'm going to make the dinner.'	She said she .... the dinner.
5 'I'll help you with the dinner.'	She said she .... me with the dinner.
6 'I'm not making the dinner.'	She said she .... the dinner.
7 'I haven't made the dinner.'	She said she .... the dinner.
8 'I made the dinner last week.'	She said she .... the dinner last week.

2 Reported speech with *say* and *tell*
Ⓖ→ 21, 22

Read the text and <u>underline</u> the right words.

Last week our history teacher ¹*said / told* that she ²*wants / wanted* us to find some photos from the 1950s. My grandfather lent me some great photos of him and my grandmother in 1957. He ³*said / told* that I ⁴*will / would* have to be careful with them, because they ⁵*were / had been* very precious to him. But on the way to school, I lost them! When I got home, I felt terrible. I knew Grandad would be upset. Then a woman came to the door – and in her hand she had the photos. She ⁶*said / told* me she ⁷*would find / had found* them in the street. She ⁸*said / told* that she ⁹*knows / had known* my grandfather for many years and that she ¹⁰*has / had* recognised his face in the photos. I was so relieved!

3 Key expressions *Everyday expressions*

Complete the conversations. Use words from box A and box B.

Ⓐ Have a   Enjoy   Nice   I had   Help

Ⓑ a great time   yourself   yourself
to see you   good holiday

1 A: Hi, Julie.

   B: Oh hi, Mike! ....

2 A: Dad, I'm going skating with Denise, OK?

   B: OK. ....

3 A: I'm going to the Caribbean tomorrow.

   B: ....

4 A: Could I have one of these biscuits?

   B: Yes, of course. ....

5 A: It was good to see you, Steve.

   B: Thanks for inviting me. ....

   ....

4 Reading *The War of the Worlds*

Read the text. Then read the questions and circle the right answer: a, b or c.

On the evening of 30th October 1938, millions of Americans were at home listening to the radio. On the radio station WABC, a play was announced: *The War of the Worlds*, directed by Orson Welles.

The programme started with dance music, but this was suddenly interrupted by a 'newsflash'. The newsreader reported that scientists had seen unusual lights on the planet Mars. After this, the music returned.

Then there was another newsflash. The audience heard that a spaceship had landed in New Jersey. Later reports said that more spaceships had landed and hundreds of people were dead. America was being attacked by creatures from Mars!

People forgot that they were listening to a play. They thought the news was real. In New York, families hid or ran into the streets in panic. They were screaming and crying. The police received hundreds of phone calls and there were traffic jams as people tried to escape from the city.

The police contacted Orson Welles in the radio studio. At the end of the programme he announced that the news reports had been part of a play. But it was several hours before people calmed down and returned to their homes. Welles said later that he was amazed by people's response to the play and added: 'I don't think we'll choose anything like this again.'

1 *The War of the Worlds* was
 a a play on the radio.
 b a radio programme about planets.
 c a news report about a war.

2 The newsreader
 a was reporting from Mars.
 b said that something strange would happen on Mars.
 c interrupted the music.

3 In the second newsflash, the reporter said that
 a aliens had just landed on Earth.
 b the situation wasn't dangerous.
 c people had killed some of the aliens.

4 The radio audience
 a enjoyed the programme.
 b believed that the events were real.
 c knew that hundreds of people had died.

5 In New York
 a there was an attack by Martians.
 b some people couldn't escape from the Martians.
 c people thought that Martians were attacking the USA.

6 Later Orson Welles said that he
 a was happy about the programme's success.
 b was very surprised by what had happened.
 c hadn't chosen the programme.

5 Extension *Time to talk*

a It's the end of the school year and Tim has just arrived at a party. Read what he says.

TIM:
• Hello!
• Sorry I'm late.
• I've brought some CDs with me. I've got some great dance music here.
• Have you invited a lot of people?
• Great. Where shall I put my jacket?
• Thanks. Hey, I'm starving. Can I have something to eat?

🔊 Now listen to the conversation.

b Read Tim's sentences again. Then imagine he's talking to you. Think about the answers <u>you</u> want to make.

c 🔊 Close your book, listen to the sentences and respond.

'Messages': Vocabulary check

1 Look at the words in the box. Find three words with the same stress pattern as *current*.

| give up | current | tiny | payment | regularly | pick up | float | pirate | grow up | marine scientist |

●● .... *current* ....

2 When you read these sentences, what words do you think of?
Choose words from the box in Exercise 1.

1   The smallest frog lives in Cuba. It's only one centimetre long!   ....

2   I never miss my karate class. I go every week.   ....

3   You can't swim here. The sea's very dangerous.   ....

4   In the past, ships were often attacked in the Caribbean.   ....

5   I remember Megan when she was a baby. Now she's at university!   ....

6   Oh no! I've dropped all my money on the floor.   ....

7   I'd like to study the plants and animals that live in the sea.   ....

8   Kelly worked at the shop on Saturday morning. They gave her £20.   ....

9   Rory used to smoke, but he's stopped now.   ....

10   If a balloon lands on the water, it doesn't sink.   ....

3 Translate these sentences into your language.

1   A: Can I borrow some of your DVDs?
    B: Yes. Help yourself.

    ....

    ....

2   Harry said he'd had a great time in London.

    ....

    ....

3   A: I can't afford a pizza for lunch. I'm broke.
    B: I'll lend you some money, but I'll have to go to
       the cashpoint.

    ....

    ....

4   A: Did anyone phone?
    B: Yes, Mel rang. She said she wanted to talk to you.

    ....

    ....

5   Our neighbours were annoyed, so I told them we'd
    turn down the music.

    ....

    ....

6   A: Whose books are these on the floor?
    B: They're mine. Don't worry, I'll pick them up.

    ....

    ....

Unit 12 Learning diary

Date _____

Now I know how to:

	Easy	Not bad	Difficult
report what people say.	☐	☐	☐

('I'm waiting for someone.') *He said he was* _____ .

('Your results aren't good enough.') *She said my* _____ .

('I saw your sister in town.') *She said* _____ .

('I haven't had an invitation.') *He said* _____ .

('I'll do it later.') *She said* _____ .

	Easy	Not bad	Difficult
use *say* and *tell* correctly in reported speech.	☐	☐	☐

I _____ *my teacher that I wasn't feeling very well.*

Kate _____ *she would like to see you.*

He _____ *his father had got a new job.*

	Easy	Not bad	Difficult
use some everyday expressions.	☐	☐	☐

Hi, Alan! Nice _____ .

I'm going to Greece tomorrow.   Have _____ .

Could I have some more rice?   Help _____ .

I'm going out with some friends tonight.   Enjoy _____ .

Did you enjoy yourself in London?   Yes, I had _____ .

	Easy	Not bad	Difficult
write formal and informal messages.	☐	☐	☐

KEY WORDS

Words connected with money

<u>lend</u> _____

_____

_____

_____

_____

_____

_____

_____

WORD WORK

Phrasal verbs

find out _____ (in my language)

give up _____

grow up _____

pick up _____

put on _____

take off _____

take out _____

turn down _____

turn off _____

turn on _____

Grammar notes*

Present simple

1 We use the present simple

- to talk about habits and regular activities.
  - He **talks** about cars all the time.
  - I **don't drink** coffee in the evening.
- to talk about general facts.
  - It **gets** dark early here in winter.
  - Sharks **don't** often **attack** people.
- with these verbs: *agree, believe, belong, forget, hate, know, like, mean, own, remember, seem, suppose, understand, want.*

We don't usually use these verbs in the present continuous.

- I **know** a lot of people in the USA. (NOT ~~I'm knowing~~)
- What **do** you **want** to eat?

Present continuous

2 We use the present continuous to talk about:

- actions that are in progress now.
  - Tara is in the kitchen. She's **having** breakfast.
  - Where are the children? What **are** they **doing**?
  - I'm **not watching** the film. You can turn the TV off.
- temporary situations.
  - Tim is at university. He's **studying** physics.
  - My uncle **is writing** a book about English castles.
- arrangements for the future.
  - We're **leaving** at 8 o'clock tomorrow.
  - What time **are** you **meeting** Colin?

Present perfect and past simple

3a We use the present perfect to talk about the present results of a past event.

We use the past simple to talk about a past event.

PRESENT PERFECT
What time is it? My watch **has stopped**.

PAST SIMPLE
The old clock in the square **stopped** years ago.

3b We often use the present perfect to give a piece of news, then we use the past simple to talk about the details.

- A: I've **lost** my English book.
  B: When **did** you **lose** it?
  A: I think I **left** it on the bus yesterday.
- A: I **haven't seen** Donna today. **Have** you **seen** her?
  B: She **went** out very early this morning.

Present perfect with *just, yet, already*

4 We use *just* for something that happened a short time ago.

We use *yet* at the end of negative sentences and questions when we expect something to happen.

We use *already* for actions that were completed before now.

- Don't close the window. I've **just** opened it.
- Wait a minute. I haven't put my shoes on **yet**.
- You must speak to Alan. Have you phoned him **yet**?
- Kate isn't here. She's **already** left.

Present perfect with *for* and *since*

5a We use the present perfect + *for* and *since* to talk about situations that started in the past and are continuing now.

- I know Tim well. I've **known** him for three years. (NOT ~~I know~~ him for three years.)

5b We use *for* to give a period of time, and *since* to say when a period of time started.

- Meg has worked in Tokyo **for** six months.
- Have you been here **for** a long time?
- I haven't seen him **since** last weekend.
- I've had this bag **since** I started school.

*For verb forms, see pages 142 and 143 in the Student's Book.

Present perfect with superlative adjectives + *ever*

6 We often use the present perfect after a superlative adjective. We use *ever* to talk about a period of time up to now.

- *This is **the best** book I've **ever** read.*
- *Who's **the most interesting** person you've **ever** met?*
- *Snowboarding is **the hardest** thing I've **ever** done.*

been and *gone*

7 Note the difference between the two past participles *been* and *gone*.

- *Carmen has **been** to London.*
  (= She was in London, but now she's come back.)
- *Luigi has **gone** to London.*
  (= He's on his way to London, or he's in London now.)

Past simple and past continuous

8a We use the past simple for a completed past action or situation.

- *Clare was very upset yesterday, and she **cried** all morning.*

We use the past continuous for a past action or situation that was in progress.

- *I gave Clare some tissues because she **was crying**.*

8b We use the past continuous and the past simple together when one action was in progress and another action interrupted it.

- *The train **was leaving** when we **arrived** at the station.*
- *I **broke** a lamp while I **was doing** the housework.*

8c When one action followed another, we use the past simple for both actions.

- *When he **heard** the noise, he **jumped** out of his chair.*

used to

9 We use *used to* + verb (NOT the past continuous) to talk about activities or situations that happened regularly in the past. These things don't happen now.

- *When I was little, I **used to** play outside a lot.*
  (NOT I ~~was playing~~ outside)
  *I **didn't use to** sit in front of the TV all the time.*
- A: *My brother was crazy when he was young.*
  B: *What **did** he **use to** do?*

Past perfect

10a

AFFIRMATIVE AND NEGATIVE		
I/He/She/It/ We/You/They	had ('d) hadn't	started.

QUESTIONS AND SHORT ANSWERS		
Had	I/he/she/it/we/you/they	started?
Yes, I had. No, she hadn't. (etc.)		

We form the past perfect with *had* + past participle of the main verb.

10b We use the past perfect when we want to emphasise that one past action happened before another past action or situation.

- *I went to the garage to get my bike, but it wasn't there. Someone **had stolen** it!*
- *When Paul **had finished** his breakfast, he did the washing up.*
- *At 3 o'clock I was hungry because I **hadn't had** any lunch.*

Future: *will* and *going to*

11a We use *will/won't* + verb to talk about

– predictions for the future and future facts.

- *I think all the shops **will be** open tomorrow.*
- *We can't go surfing now. It'**ll be** dark in ten minutes and we **won't be able to** see anything.*

– things we decide to do at the moment of speaking (e.g. when we make an offer).

- A: *I'm not ready yet.*
  B: *Don't worry. I'**ll wait**.*
- A: *These glasses are dirty.*
  B: *Give them to me. I'**ll wash** them.*

11b We use *going to* + verb to talk about our intentions, things that we've already decided to do.

- A: *Have you got a ticket for the film?*
  B: *Yes. I'm going to see it next Monday.*
- A: *Do you want to come to the shopping centre with me?*
  B: *Yes, OK. What are you going to buy?*

when in future sentences

12 We use the present simple after *when* in future sentences.

- *Will you see Danny when you go into town?*
  (NOT *when you will go into town.*)
- *I'm going to finish my homework when I get to school.*

First conditional

13a

> IF + PRESENT SIMPLE + WILL/WON'T + VERB
> *If you wear boots, your feet won't get wet.*

We use the first conditional to describe the result of a possible future action.

We can put the *if* clause after the main clause.

- *If you don't wear a coat, you'll be cold.*
  You'll be cold if you don't wear a coat.

13b We can often use *unless* + a verb in the affirmative instead of *if* + a negative verb. The meaning is the same.

- *You'll be cold if you don't wear a coat.*
  You'll be cold unless you wear a coat.

Second conditional

14

> IF + PAST SIMPLE + WOULD ('D)/WOULDN'T + VERB
> *If she had a dog, she wouldn't be lonely.*

We use the second conditional when we talk about the result of a hypothetical action or situation in the present or the future.

We can put the *if* clause after the main clause.

- *If I didn't feel ill, I'd come with you.*
  I'd come with you if I didn't feel ill.

might and *may*

15 We use *might/may* + verb to describe a future action or situation that isn't certain.

Might and *may* have got the same meaning, but we usually use *might* in questions.

- *Our school might be/may be on television next week, but it isn't certain.*
- *I'll give Jack your message if I see him, but I might not see/may not see him.*
- A: *I'm worried. Linda may do something stupid.*
  B: *What might she do?*

must / have to

16 We use *must* and *have to* to talk about obligation. We can sometimes use either *must* or *have to*.

- *Hurry up! We must leave / have to leave now!*

But we normally use *must* when the speaker is giving a personal opinion, and *have to* when the obligation comes from a rule or an arrangement.

- MOTHER: *Fiona, you must stay at home this evening!*
  (A personal command.)
- FIONA: *I can't go out this evening. I have to stay at home.*
  (Her mother's rule.)

mustn't / don't have to

17 *Mustn't* and *don't have to* haven't got the same meaning.

We use *mustn't* to give orders and to say that something is necessary.

We use *don't have to* to say that something isn't necessary.

- *You mustn't eat all that! You'll be ill.*
  (= Don't eat all that!)
- *You don't have to eat all that if you aren't hungry.*
  (= You can eat it if you like, but it isn't necessary.)

Speculation: *must / can't / might / could*

18 We use *must* + verb when we're sure that something is true.

- A: *I don't think Alice knows Nick.*
  B: *She **must know** him. They're in the same class.*

We use *can't* + verb when we're sure that something is impossible.

- A: *I'm going to swim to the island.*
  B: *You **can't be** serious. It's 3 kilometres!*

We use *might* or *could* + verb when we think that something is possible.

- A: *Where's Zak?*
  B: *He **might be** at home, or he **could be** at Dave's house.*

should / shouldn't

19 We use *should / shouldn't* + verb to give advice, to say that we think something is or isn't the right thing to do.

- A: *I found this silver necklace in the street. What **should** I **do**?*
  B: *You **should take** it to the police station.*
  C: *You **shouldn't keep** it.*
  D: *You **should put** an advert in the local newspaper.*

The passive: present simple / past simple

20a We use the passive when it isn't important to say who or what does / did an action.

- *Japanese cars **are sold** all over the world.* (We aren't interested in who sells the cars.)
- *Rice **isn't grown** in Britain.*
- *The old church **was destroyed** in 1944.*
- *The boys **weren't hurt** in the accident.*

20b We can use *by* in a passive sentence to say who or what did the action.

- *This photo **was taken by** my grandfather fifty years ago.*

Reported speech

21a When we report what someone said, we often make these changes:

present tense → past tense
present perfect → past perfect
past simple → past perfect
will → would

We often leave out *that* before a reported statement.

Direct speech	Reported speech
'I **like** my job.'	He said (that) he **liked** his job.
'I'm **feeling** ill.'	She said (that) she **was feeling** ill.
'We **haven't seen** the film.'	They said (that) they **hadn't seen** the film.
'I **saw** a man near the car.'	He said (that) he **had seen** a man near the car.
'Mel **will be** here soon.'	She said (that) Mel **would be** here soon.

21b Note that pronouns and possessive adjectives often change in reported speech.

- *'I like **my** job.'*
  *He said (that) **he** liked **his** job.*

say and tell

22 To introduce reported speech, we use *tell*, and not *say*, when we mention the person we're speaking to.

- *You **told me** you didn't like mushrooms.*
- *You **said** you didn't like mushrooms.*
  (NOT *You said me you didn't like mushrooms.*)

want / ask / tell someone to do something

23 Note the word order here:

want / ask / tell + noun or object pronoun (*me, her*, etc.) + *to* + verb

- A: *What do you **want me to** do?*
  B: *I **want you to** do the shopping.*
- *When Kate **asked her brother to** lend her some money, he **told her to** ask someone else.*

give + direct and indirect object

24a The verb *give* can have two objects: an indirect object (the person who receives something) and a direct object (the thing that someone gives).

We usually put the indirect object before the direct object:

	INDIRECT OBJECT	DIRECT OBJECT
● Jack gave	me	that DVD.
● I'll give	my sister	the photos.

But we can put the indirect object (with *to*) after the direct object:

	DIRECT OBJECT	INDIRECT OBJECT
● I'll give	the photos	to my sister.

24b When the direct object is a pronoun (*it/them*), we usually put the indirect object (with *to*) after the direct object:

	DIRECT OBJECT	INDIRECT OBJECT
● Jack gave	it	to me.
● I'll give	them	to my sister.

We must use *to* here. (NOT *Jack gave it me.*)

24c We use the same constructions with the verbs *lend, show, pass, send.*

- I lent Colin €10.
- Can you pass me the salt?
- Show this photo to all your friends.
- Send it to them by email.

The *-ing* form

25a When the verbs *enjoy, can't stand, don't / doesn't mind* are followed by another verb, we use the *-ing* form of the second verb, and we usually do the same after *like, love, hate, prefer.*

- I don't mind **spending** time on my own, but I prefer **being** with my friends.
- Do you like **living** here?

NB We don't use the *-ing* form after *would like/would prefer/would hate.*

- I'd like **to be** an actor.

25b We use the *-ing* form after prepositions.

- I'm interested **in cooking**.
- I'm not very good **at making** decisions.

Verbs + prepositions

26 With prepositional verbs (*think about, look at,* etc.), the preposition comes at the end of the sentence in questions with *What* and *Who.*

- A: I'm thinking **about** someone.
  B: Who are you thinking **about**?
- A: He's looking **at** something.
  B: What's he looking **at**?
- A: I'm listening **to** something.
  B: What are you listening **to**?
- A: I'm waiting for someone.
  B: Who are you waiting **for**?

Subject and object questions with *Who* and *What*

27 *Who* and *What* can be the subject or the object of a verb. When they're the object, we use *do/does/did* with the verb.

SUBJECT
- **Who phoned** you?
  (<u>Someone</u> phoned you.)
- **What's happening**?
  (<u>Something's</u> happening.)

OBJECT
- **Who did** you **phone**?
  (You phoned <u>someone</u>.)
- **What do** you **want**?
  (You want <u>something</u>.)

so and *neither*

28a When we want to say that we feel the same or that we do the same as the speaker, we use *so/neither* + auxiliary verb in the affirmative + *I.*

We use *so* after an affirmative statement and *neither* after a negative statement.

- A: I'm leaving now.
  B: So **am** I.
- A: I **can't** swim.
  B: Neither **can** I.

28b After the present simple or the past simple we use *do/does/did*.

- A: *I **hate** doing the washing up.*
  B: *So **do** I.*
- A: *I **didn't** like that film.*
  B: *Neither **did** I.*

Contradictions

29 We can use short answers to contradict someone.

- A: *You're lazy.*
  B: ***No, I'm not!***
  A: ***Yes, you are!*** *You sit in front of the television all evening.*
  B: ***No, I don't!***
  A: ***Yes, you do!***

Relative clauses with *who/that/which*

30 We use relative clauses beginning with *who, that* or *which* to identify which person or thing we're talking about.

We use *who* or *that* for people, and *that* or *which* for things.

- *Can you see the man **who's/that's** wearing sunglasses?*
- *There are lots of trains **that/which** go to London.*

For things, we use *that* more often than *which*.

one/ones

31 We use *one/ones* to avoid repeating a noun:

- after an adjective:
- A: *I'd like three large bottles of water.*
  B: *I've only got **two large ones**. Do you want **a small one** as well?*
  (NOT ~~two large~~ or ~~a small~~)
- after *the*:
- *Can you see those boys, **the ones** that are sitting on the bench?*
- *The best restaurant is **the one** in Mill Street.*

Comparatives and superlatives

32a For adjectives with one syllable, we add *-er* or *-r* for the comparative, and *the* + *-est* or *-st* for the superlative.

- (tall) *I'm **taller** than my brother.*
- (large) *Anacondas are **the largest** snakes in the world.*

When the adjective ends in 1 vowel + 1 consonant, we double the consonant.
*big – **bigger**/**the biggest***
*hot – **hotter**/**the hottest***

32b For most adjectives with two or more syllables, we use *more* and *the most* before the adjective.

- *You must be **more careful**.*
- *Is the film **more exciting** than the book?*
- *Football is **the most popular** sport in Britain.*

32c But for two-syllable adjectives ending in consonant + *y*, we use *ier/iest*.

- (easy) *It's **easier** if you go by train.*
- (lazy) *My cat's **the laziest** cat in the world.*

32d Note these irregular comparative and superlative forms.

- (good) ***better**/**the best***
- (bad) ***worse**/**the worst***

less/fewer/more

33 The comparative forms *less* and *fewer* are the opposite of *more*.

We use *less* with uncountable nouns (*noise, crime*, etc.) and *fewer* with countable nouns (*people, cars*, etc.).

We use *more* with countable and uncountable nouns.

- *I like going to the beach in the evening. There are **fewer people** and **less noise**.*
- *Most people would like **more holidays** and **more free time**.*

any and no + noun

34 We use *any* + noun with a verb in the negative, and *no* + noun with a verb in the affirmative. The meaning is the same.

We can use uncountable and plural nouns after *any* and *no*.

- I haven't got **any** money.
  I've got **no** money.

- There aren't **any** free seats on the train.
  There are **no** free seats on the train.

Adverbs of manner

35 We use adverbs of manner to describe a verb, to say <u>how</u> an action is done.

- I listened **carefully** to the instructions.

We form most adverbs of manner by adding *ly* to the adjective:

slow – slowly   careful – carefully   safe – safely

But note these spelling changes:

- *easy – eas**ily** (y after a consonant – ily)*

- *comfortable – comfortab**ly** (le – ly)*

- *enthusiastic – enthusias**tically** (ic – ically)*

A few adverbs have got the same form as the adjective, e.g. *hard, early, fast, late.*

- He works **hard**.

- I got up **late** this morning.

so + adjective / such + a/an + noun

36 To emphasise something, we use *so* before an adjective.

- Let's go home. This party's **so boring**!

We use *such a/an* before a noun or an adjective + a noun.

- You're **such a liar**! That isn't true.

- He's **such an interesting person**!

After *so ...* or *such ...* we can add a clause.

- The party was **so boring that** I went home.

- It was **such a long journey that** I fell asleep in the car.

too / enough

37 We use *too* + adjective/adverb to say that something is 'more than necessary'.

- Don't buy those shoes. They're **too expensive**.

- Be careful! You're driving **too fast**.

We use adjective/adverb + *enough* to say that something is/isn't sufficient.

- Try these shoes. I think they're **big enough**.

- He's lazy. He doesn't work **hard enough**.

Phrasal verbs

38 Phrasal verbs are two-word verbs (*go out, take off, turn down,* etc.).

- I think I'll **go out** tonight.

When a phrasal verb has got a noun object, we can put it before or after the second part of the verb (*out, off, down,* etc.).

But a pronoun object (*it, them*) always goes before the second part of the verb.

- Take off **your shoes**.
  Take **your shoes** off.
  Take **them** off. (NOT Take ~~off them.~~)

- Can you turn down **the radio**?
  Can you turn **the radio** down?
  Can you turn **it** down?
  (NOT Can you ~~turn down it?~~)